COMPANY LAW- SUPREME COURT'S LEADING CASE LAWS

CASE NOTES- FACTS- FINDINGS OF APEX COURT JUDGES & CITATIONS

JAYPRAKASH BANSILAL SOMANI

Copyright © Jayprakash Bansilal Somani
All Rights Reserved.

Dedicated

To

All the Past & Present Judges of the Supreme Court of India.

Salute to their wisdom.

Salute to their interpretation of Law.

Salute to their elaborative judgement writing.

Contents

Contents

Preface

Dear Learned Advocates of the NCLT, NCLAT, CA, CS, IPs, High Courts, Supreme Court, Corporates & Individuals,

I am very delighted to provide you a book on 'COMPANY LAW-Supreme Court of India's Leading Case Laws'.

In this book you will get...

1. Name of the Case i. e. Cause title

2. Relevant Sections discussed in the case

3. Hon'ble Judges/Coram of the case

4. Number of PDF Pages in Original Judgement of the case

5. All available Citations of the case

6. Case Note with appeal allowed/ dismissed or disposed off

7. Facts of the case

8. Hon'ble Apex Court's findings, while dismissing/allowing or disposing the appeal

9. Ratio Decidendi if any.

My special thanks to Manupatra, because of their web portal I can compile this book in well manner. I am also thankful to Notion Press to support me to publish & market this book throughout the Country. Thanks to my Juniors, Advocate Colleagues & Insolvency Professional Colleagues to support me in this venture.

Mr. Rachit Manchanda has helped me a lot to compile this book.

I hope this book will add some value addition in the wealth of your legal knowledge. Your positive feedbacks will boost me to compile/ write further books & negative feedbacks will improve my skills. Kindly send your valuable feedbacks by email.

Thanks with Regards,

Jayprakash B. Somani

Advocate, Supreme Court of India

Email: jaysomani64@gmail.com

Web Site: www.jayprakashsomani.com

Call: 8384051134, 9322188701, 9318381287

Acknowledgements

Printed & Published by
Notion Press
No. 8, 3rd Cross Street,
CIT Colony, Mylapore,
Chennai, Tamil Nadu- 600004

Managed by
Jayprakash Somani Advocates & Solicitors
Law Firm for Supreme Court of India
Delhi Office
257 C, Pocket 1, Mayur Vihar Phase 1, Delhi 110091.
Call 8384051134, 9322188701, 8459194576, 9318381287
01141051516
Supreme Court Chamber
312, 3rd Floor, M. C. Setalvad Block, In front of 'D' Gate, Bhagwan Das
Road, Supreme Court of India, New Delhi 110001
Contact: 8459194576, 9811011747,
www.jayprakashsomani.com

Books are available online at
1. Notion Press: https://notionpress.com/author/jayprakash_somani
2. Amazon: https://www.amazon.in/s?k=jayprakash+somani
3.   Flipkart: https://www.flipkart.com/
search?q=Jayprakash%20Somani

CHAPTER ONE

Raheja Universal Limited vs. NRC Limited and Ors. 2012

Hon'ble Judges/Coram:

S.H. Kapadia, C.J.I., K.S. Panicker Radhakrishnan and Swatanter Kumar, JJ

Relevant Sections:

Companies Act, 1956 – Section 391, Section 394

Equivalent Citations:

AIR2012SC1440, I(2012)BC686, 2012(2)CTC102, 2012(4)SCC148, MANU/SC/0177/2012

No of pages in the original judgment: 2

Case Notes:

SICA - Jurisdiction - Sections 17, 18, 22A, 22(1), 22(3) and 22(4) of Sick Industrial Companies (Special Provisions) Act, 1985; Sections 53A and 54 of Transfer of Property Act, 1882 - High Court quashed order of Authority for Industrial and Financial Reconstruction and confirmed order passed by Board for Industrial and Financial Restructuring (BIFR) - Hence, present Appeals - Whether an agreement to sell in relation to an immovable property transferred or created any right or title in immovable property itself in favour of purchaser - Whether in facts and circumstances of case, BIFR had jurisdiction to issue a direction or make a declaration in relation to agreement in question in exercise of powers vested in it under Section 22(3) of Act 1985

Brief Facts:

Memorandum of understanding and agreement to sell land belonging to company between Appellant and Respondent-company was signed prior to presentation of scheme before BIFR - Once asset of Company and/or its sale proceeds had been integral part of formation and finalization of revival scheme, such transaction by any stretch of imagination could not be stated to be beyond ambit and scope of Section 22(3) of Act 1985 - Thus, BIFR had power to issue declarations in relation to contracts, agreements, settlements, awards, standing orders or even other instruments in force to which sick industrial company was a party - Power to suspend or power to enforce same subject to such adaptations as BIFR might consider appropriate was a power of great magnitude and scope, only restriction thereupon was as contemplated in proviso to Section 22(3) of Act 1985 - Provisions of Section 53A of 1882 Act, recognized a right of a transferee, where a transferor had given and transferee had taken possession of property or any part thereof - This provision did not create title of transferee in property in question but gave him a very limited right, that too, subject to satisfaction of conditions as stated in Section 53A of Act of 1882 itself - Thus, even if part performance of agreement was accepted, still no title was created in favour of Respondent-Company - Provisions of Section 53A would also not, in any way, alter position of Act 1985 having an overriding effect vis-à-vis provisions of Act 1882 - Provisions of Act of 1985 would have precedence and overriding effect over provisions of Act 1882 - BIFR issued a prohibitory order requiring secured creditors not to take any coercive steps against company without prior permission of BIFR - This order of BIFR was passed at stage of consideration of revival scheme which had been approved by CDR Group as well as secured creditors - Land was paramount asset of Company for its revival and successful implementation of scheme in accordance with law - Asset was duly taken into consideration in formulation of scheme as contemplated under Sections 17 and 18 of Act 1985 and appropriate directions, prohibitory orders were issued within ambit and scope of Sections 22(1), 22(3) and 22A of Act 1985 - It could not be said that, BIFR had no jurisdiction to pass such directives - Land being primary asset of Respondent-Company, could not be permitted to be dissolved by sale or otherwise without consent and approval of BIFR - BIFR was authority proprio vigore and required to oversee entire affairs of a sick industrial company and to ensure that same were within framework of scheme formulated and approved by Board for revival of company in accordance with provisions of Act 1985

Held while dismissing the appeal,

Held, Section 54 of 1882 Act, defined 'Sale' as a transfer of ownership in exchange for price paid or promised or part-paid and part promised - Such a transfer of tangible immovable property of value of Rs. 100 and upwards could be made only by a registered instrument - An agreement for sale or an agreement to sell itself did not create any interest or charge in such property - A mere contract for sale of immovable property did not create any interest in immovable property - Memorandum of understanding and agreement to sell land belonging to company between Appellant and Respondent-company was signed prior to presentation of scheme before BIFR - Once asset of Company and/or its sale proceeds had been integral part of formation and finalization of revival scheme, such transaction by any stretch of imagination could not be stated to be beyond ambit and scope of Section 22(3) of Act 1985 - Thus, BIFR had power to issue declarations in relation to contracts, agreements, settlements, awards, standing orders or even other instruments in force to which sick industrial company was a party - Power to suspend or power to enforce same subject to such adaptations as BIFR might consider appropriate was a power of great magnitude and scope, only restriction thereupon was as contemplated in proviso to Section 22(3) of Act 1985 - Provisions of Section 53A of 1882 Act, recognized a right of a transferee, where a transferor had given and transferee had taken possession of property or any part thereof - This provision did not create title of transferee in property in question but gave him a very limited right, that too, subject to satisfaction of conditions as stated in Section 53A of Act of 1882 itself - Thus, even if part performance of agreement was accepted, still no title was created in favour of Respondent-Company - Provisions of Section 53A would also not, in any way, alter position of Act 1985 having an overriding effect vis-à-vis provisions of Act 1882 - Provisions of Act of 1985 would have precedence and overriding effect over provisions of Act 1882 - BIFR issued a prohibitory order requiring secured creditors not to take any coercive steps against company without prior permission of BIFR - This order of BIFR was passed at stage of consideration of revival scheme which had been approved by CDR Group as well as secured creditors - Land was paramount asset of Company for its revival and successful implementation of scheme in accordance with law - Asset was duly taken into consideration in formulation of scheme as contemplated under Sections 17 and 18 of Act 1985 and appropriate directions, prohibitory orders were issued within ambit and scope of Sections 22(1), 22(3) and 22A of Act 1985 - It could not be said that, BIFR had no jurisdiction to pass such directives - Land being primary asset of Respondent-Company, could not be permitted to be dissolved by sale or otherwise without consent and approval of BIFR -

BIFR was authority proprio vigore and required to oversee entire affairs of a sick industrial company and to ensure that same were within framework of scheme formulated and approved by Board for revival of company in accordance with provisions of Act 1985 - Neither BIFR nor High Court had exceeded its jurisdiction in passing impugned orders - Once scheme was implemented or period specified under provisions of Sections 22(3) and 22(4) of Act expired, then declaration would cease to exist and Appellant would be entitled to enforce its rights in accordance with law as if no such declaration or restriction ever existed - A scheme for rehabilitation or restructuring of a sick industrial company undertaken by a specialized body like BIFR/AAIFR should, as far as legally permissible, remain obstruction free and events should take place as pre-ordained, during consideration and successful implementation of formulated scheme - Wide jurisdiction was vested in BIFR/AAIFR to issue directives, declarations and prohibitory orders within rationalized scope and limitations prescribed under Section 22(1), 22(3) and 22A of Act 1985 - Order of BIFR, which had merged into order of High Court was maintained and order of Authority for Industrial and Financial Reconstruction was set aside - Appeals dismissed

CHAPTER TWO

Rajinder Kumar Malhotra and Ors. Vs. Company Law Board and Ors., 1994

Hon'ble Judges/Coram: M.N. Venkatachaliah, C.J. and S. Mohan, J.

Relevant Sections:

Companies Act, 1956 - Section 397, Companies Act, 1956 - Section 398

Equivalent Citation:

1996 85CompCas176(SC), 1995 3 CompLJ53(SC), ,1995Supp(1)SCC530, 1995(1)SCALE210, MANU/SC/0943/1995

Number of pages in the original judgement:2

Case Note:

Company - Collaboration - Sections 397 and 398 of Companies Act, 1956 - Petitioners/shareholders claimed that collaboration arrangement of company was illegal and operated as oppression of minority - High Court passed order, which partially stayed operation of an interlocutory order of Company Law Board - Hence, this Petition - Whether, constructions of Boards order was unnecessary - Held, Directions of Board could not be continued as coming in way of Respondents' taking all such antecedent preliminary and preparatory steps, short of issuing shares to collaborator - Approval of shareholders for issue of shares to collaborating company was concerned, matter would abide decision of members at general meeting - Thus, construction of Board's order makes proceedings before High Court was unnecessary - Objection being affected, it observed that if there were orders made in other proceedings in this behalf observations in this order would not had been effected of nullifying them - All that need be said was that Board had not interdicted such preparatory steps - Thus, Respondents may find no need to proceed with Petition before High Court - As earlier order of stay of this Court stands vacated - Petition disposed of.

Brief Facts:

We have heard Sri G. Ramaswamy, learned senior Counsel for the petitioners and Sri K.K. Venugopal and Sri Ashok Desai, learned senior Counsel for the respondents. Petitioners claim to be a minority shareholder in the company and respondents are the company and its other directors and shareholders.

It was urged before the Board by the petitioners that the collaboration arrangement embarked upon by the said company with M/s. Gillette was illegal and operated as oppression of the minority. The Company Law Board by its order dated 20th October, 1993 noticed the prayers made before it:

(a) Respondent No. 1 company should not approve of any transfer of its shares;

(b) Adequate notice be given to the petitioners for any general meeting of the shareholders;

(c) Respondents 11, 12 and 13 be restrained from changing their management as they had nearly 58% of the share capital of respondent No. 1;

(d) Respondent No. 1 company be restrained from making any fresh issue of shares.

Held while disposing off the appeal,

In view of this clarification, the respondents may find no need to proceed with the writ petition before the Calcutta High Court. That petition is withdrawn to this Court and is disposed of accordingly. A formal order in this behalf shall be made by the High Court.

8. The earlier order of stay of this Court stands vacated. The special leave petition is disposed of accordingly.

Ratio Decidendi:

"When approval of shareholders for issue of shares to collaborate company is concerned, then matter will abide decision of members at general meeting"

CHAPTER THREE

IDBI Bank Limited vs. The Official Liquidator, Office of the Official Liquidator of Companies and Ors., 2019

Hon'ble Judges/Coram:

Mohan M. Shantanagoudar and Ajay Rastogi, JJ

Relevant Section:

Companies Act, 1956 - Section 531

Equivalent Citation:

2020 (15)SC517, 2019(14)SCALE596, 2020-2-LW653, 2020(5)CTC849, MANU/SC/1457/2019

Number of pages in the Judgement: 3

Case Note:

Company - Execution of deed - Winding up proceedings - Section 531 of Companies Act, 1956 and Rules 24,96,99 and 101 of Companies Rules, 1959 - One company availed working capital loan from Petitioner and defaulted on same - Towards one time settlement, said company offered to sell its property-Office Space - Pursuant to same, said company and Petitioner executed agreement to sell with respect to subject property - Respondent No. 3 preferred company petitions seeking winding up of company and repayment of their dues - Company Judge issued directions for appointment of Administrator and Provisional Liquidator for company - Petitioner filed Company Application to execute sale deed in its favour for subject property and to dismiss winding up petition- Company Judge dismissed applications - On appeal, Division Bench of High Court dismissed application seeking execution of sale deed in favour of Petitioner and also revived winding up proceedings - Hence, present appeal - Whether Division Bench was correct in reviving winding up proceedings and Petitioner had right to seek execution of sale deed in its favour.

Brief Facts:

One company availed a working capital loan from the Petitioner and defaulted on the same. Consequently, it proposed a one-time settlement to the Petitioner for repayment of its dues. Towards this end, said company offered to sell its property-Office Space. Pursuant to the same, company and the Petitioner executed an agreement to sell with respect to the subject property for a consideration. Respondent No. 3 preferred company petitions under Section 433(e) and (f) and Section 434 of the Companies Act, 1956 seeking the winding up of company and the repayment of their dues. The Company Judge issued directions for appointment of an Administrator and a Provisional Liquidator for company. The Petitioner filed Company Application in winding up petition, seeking a direction to the Administrator to execute a sale deed in its favour for the subject property, as per Section 536(2) of the 1956 Act and also dismissed winding up petition. On appeal, the Division Bench of High Court dismissed application seeking execution of sale deed in favour of Petitioner and also revived winding up proceedings.

Held,while dismissing the petition:

(i) Winding up proceedings are proceedings in rem and have an impact on the rights of people, in general. Thus, it was mandatory to advertise such proceedings, so as to ensure that they receive the widest possible publicity and all relevant stakeholders have adequate notice. This implies that in a situation where the petitioning creditor fails to advertise the petition and no other creditor or contributory comes forward to prosecute it, Rule 101 should not be read in a manner that absolutely bars the continuation of a winding up petition. This was particularly so when there are unsatisfied creditors who should have been given an opportunity to prosecute the petition, but were deprived of the same due to the failure to advertise. Indeed, Rule 101 was only limited to instances where the petitioning creditor fails to advertise the petition. However, there was nothing in the language of Rules 24, 96, or 99 to indicate that only such petitioning creditor could advertise the petition. Given the absence of a specific provision mandating that the petition only be advertised by petitioning creditor, the Company Court had the discretion to direct the publishing of an advertisement to secure the interest of other creditors. In such situations, the winding up proceedings could not be dismissed, as it would frustrate the very objective of securing the interest of all creditors. [11.3]

(ii) It would be unjust to dismiss the winding up petition in the instant case solely on the ground that there was no other person willing to substitute the original creditor in terms of Rule 101 of Rules. Here, due to the lack of adequate advertisement of the winding up petitions, it appears that the secured creditors of company were constrained to approach the DRT for recovery of their dues by filing application. Further, upon learning of the decision of the Company Judge dismissing the winding up petition, one of the secured creditors also approached the DRT to secure its interest. Based on this, the DRT had directed that the amount to be returned to company be attached so that the banks have an opportunity to recover their dues from company. This clearly goes on to show that the secured creditors of company were relevant stakeholders who were affected by the non-advertising of the winding up petition. They should have been called upon to indicate whether they would want to step into the shoes of the petitioning creditors as per Rule 101 of Rules. [11.4]

(iii) It appear that the Division Bench had entirely ignored the second requirement under Section 531 of Act. Solely based on an examination of factors indicating a dominant motive of the management of company to benefit the Petitioner, it went on to hold that the agreement to sell constitutes a fraudulent preference. In doing so, it had failed to appreciate that the said agreement was executed, while the winding up petitions were filed, signifying that there was a gap of over sixteen months between the two events, as opposed to the six-month period contemplated under Section 531 of Act. Similarly, it failed to consider that even the transfer of possession of the subject property occurred, which was also before the six-month period preceding the filing of the winding up petition. Clearly then, the Division Bench had erred in ignoring the time limit stipulated under Section 531 of Act and holding that the transaction qualifies as a fraudulent preference. The same could not be disregarded as it was crucial for ensuring commercial certainty for parties transacting with a company. [17.3]

(iv) Therefore, it was evident that the agreement to sell could not be termed as a fraudulent preference under Section 531 of Act. [17.5]

CHAPTER FOUR

Bajaj Auto Ltd. vs. Company Law Board and Ors., 1998

Hon'ble Judges/Coram:

B.N. Kirpal and S.S.M. Quadri, JJ.

Relevant Section:

Companies Act, 1956 - Section 108A, Companies Act, 1956 - Section 111, Companies Act, 1956 - Section 82; Monopolies And Restrictive Trade Practices Act, 1969 [repealed] - Section 2(g), Section 20(a), Section 25, Section 26

Equivalent Citation:

1998VAD(SC)408, AIR1999SC345, [1998]30CLA195(SC), [1999]95CompCas12(SC), (1998)3CompLJ366(SC), JT1998(5)SC114, 1998(4)SCALE250, (1998)6SCC218, [1998]3SCR881, MANU/SC/0437/1998

Number of pages in the original judgement: 8

Case Note:

Company - transfer of shares - there is nothing on record to show that purchase of shares by appellants was with ulterior or oblique motives and purposes - appellants do not intend to destablish management of company in question - acquisition in question would not lead to inter-connection between company of appellant and company in question - power exercised by directors of company in question in refusing transfer of shares was not bona fide or in interest of company or general body of share holders

Brief Facts:

Bajaj Auto Limited (appellant in Civil Appeal No. 3480/86) is the holding company of Bajaj Auto Holdings Limited (appellant in C.A. Nos. 3480/86 & 3420-79/86) and they, along with other individuals who were members of their group (all of whom are appellants in these appeals, are existing share-holders of Bajaj Tempo Limited which is a public Limited company. Bajaj Auto Limited purchased SO shares of Bajaj Tempo Limited and Bajaj Auto Holdings Limited purchased 13150 shares of the said company. These purchases were made in the year 1983 through different brokers and they were sent to M/s. Bajaj Tempo Limited for transfer of shares in the appellants' names. By three different resolutions dated 29.8.1983,27.9.1983 and 19.11.1983, the transfer of shares was rejected by Bajaj Tempo Limited.

Held,

For the aforesaid reasons, the appeals are allowed. The impugned order dated 28.7.1986 of the Company Law Board is set aside and the Resolutions dated 29.8.1983,27.9.1983 and 19.11.1-983 of M/s. Bajaj Tempo Limited are set-aside and as a consequence thereof, direction is given to respondent No. 2 to register the shares in question within four weeks from the date of this judgment. The appellants will be entitled to cost.

Ratio Decidendi:

"When approval of shareholders for issue of shares to collaborate company is concerned, then matter will abide decision of members at general meeting"

CHAPTER FIVE

Rampur Distillery and Chemical Co. Ltd. and Ors. vs. Company Law Board and Ors., 1969

Hon'ble Judges/Coram:
J.C. Shah, Vaidynathier Ramaswami and A.N. Grover, JJ.
Relevant Section:
COMPANIES ACT, 1956 - Section 326, Section 330
Number of pages in original judgement:3
Case Note:

Company - managing agent - Sections 10, 326, 326 (2) and 330 of Companies Act, 1956 - company appointed managing agent for 20 years in 1946 - information lodged by Registrar that director of managing agency had committed offences of criminal breach of trust - police lodged criminal complaint against director - application for extension of term of managing agency made by company - application was rejected by Company Law Board - whether managing agency is person in eyes of law and fit to be re-appointed in capacity of managing agent - past conduct of agency was relevant to be taken into account while deciding issue of re-appointment - Board had to consider entire past or present conduct of directors of agency - Company Law Board assured Court that with help of company Board will take step to dispose of matter.

Brief Facts:

The Rampur Distillery Company Ltd. hereinafter called the Rampur Company' is a manufacturer of industrial alcohol. In 1943 the Rampur

Company appointed Govan Brothers its managing agent for 20 years. In July 1946 a group of persons who may be referred to as the 'Dalmia Group' assumed control over Govan Brothers. V.H. Dalmia who became Managing Director of Govan Brothers, besides being a director of a number of other companies, held important position in several trade associations. On March 19, 1953, information was lodged by the Registrar of Joint Stock Companies, Delhi, that V.H. Dalmia and others had committed offences of criminal breach on trust.

2. By virtue of Section 330 of the Companies Act, 1956, the Managing agency of the Rampur Company was to expire on August 15, 1960, unless before that date the managing agent was re-appointed for a fresh term in accordance with the provisions of the Companies Act. On December 10, 1959 the Rampur Company re-appointed Govan Brothers, Managing' Agent for ten years with effect from August 15, 1960, and applied to the Central Government that the extension of the managing agency of Govan Brothers be approved. The Central Government granted extension for five years under Section 326 of the Companies Act with effect from August 15, 1960.

Held while dismissing the appeal,

The appeal filed by the Rampur Company must therefore fail. It must, however, be pointed out that the time during which the managing agency of Govan Brothers is to remain Krishna v. Sarvagna Krishna {Prs. [1920] S.C.1795 in operation is fast running out. The Solicitor-General appearing on behalf of the Company Law Board and the Union of India have assured us that with the co-operation of the Rampur Company, the Board will take steps to dispose of the application within one month from the date on which the order reaches the Company Law Board.

The appeals fail and are dismissed. There will be no order as to costs in this Court.

CHAPTER SIX

The Barium Chemicals Ltd. and Ors. vs. The Company Law Board and Ors., 1966

Hon'ble Judges/Coram:

A.K. Sarkar, C.J., J.M. Shelat, J.R. Mudholkar, M. Hidayatullah and R.S. Bachawat, JJ.

Relevant Section:

Companies Act, 1956 - Sections 10B, 10E, 27, 234, 235 to 251

Equivalent Citation:

AIR1967SC295, [1966]36CompCas639(SC), (1966)2CompLJ151(SC), [1967]1SCR898, [1966]SuppSCR311, MANU/SC/0037/1966

Number of pages in original judgement:6

Case Note:

Company - investigation - Sections 10B, 10E, 27, 234, 235 to 251 of Companies Act, 1956 - inspector appointed under Section 237 (b) to investigate affairs of appellant-company - validity of Order challenged on grounds that it was mala fide and Company Law Board (CLB) acted on materials extraneous to Section 237 (b) - respondent contended that there was delay, bungling and faulty planning of projects, share capital being wiped out so investigation was essential - Apex Court opined these circumstances cannot by themselves suggest an intent to defraud or fraudulent management - mere bungling or faulty planning cannot constitute misfeasance or misconduct - where circumstances set out in Section 237 (b) do not exist then opinion of CLB can be challenged on ground of non-application of mind or perversity on grounds that it formed collateral grounds and was beyond scope of the statute.

Brief Facts:

On May 19, 1965 Mr. D. S. Dang, Secretary of the Company Law Board issued an order on behalf of the Company Law Board made under s. 237(b) of the Companics Act, 1956 appointing 4 persons as Inspectors for investigating the affairs of the Barium Chemicals Ltd., appellant No. 1 before us, since its incorporation in the year 1961 and to report to the Company Law Board inter alia "all type irregularities and contravention in respect of the provisions of the Companies Act, 1956 or of any other law for the time being in force and the person or persons responsible for such irregularities and contraventions." The order was made by the Chairman of the Board, Mr. R. C. Dutt on behalf of the Board by virtue of the powers conferred on him by certain rules to which we shall refer later. On June 4, 1965 the Company preferred a writ petition under Art. 226 of the Constitution in the Punjab High Court for the issue of a writ of mandamus or other appropriate writ, direction or order quashing the order of the Board dated May 19, 1965. The Managing Director, Mr. Balasubramanian joined in the petition as petitioner No. 2. The writ petition is directed against 7 respondents, the first of which is the Company Law Board. The second respondent is Mr. T. T. Krishnamachari, who was at that time Minister for Finance in the Government of India. The Inspectors appointed are respondents 3 to 6 and Mr. Dang is the 7th respondent. Apart from the relief of quashing the order of May 19, 1965 the appellants sought the issue of a writ restraining the Company Law Board and the Inspectors from giving effect to the order dated May 19, 1965 and also sought some other incidental reliefs

Held while aloowing the appeal,

Though the contentions regarding mala fides and the constitutional invalidity of s. 237(b) are not upheld, the appellant succeed in the other two contentions. The appeal is allowed and the impugned order is set aside. Since the appellants have partly succeeded and partly failed, there will be no order as to costs.

Jignesh Shah and Ors. vs. Union of India (UOI) and Ors. 2019

Hon'ble Judges/Coram:
Rohinton Fali Nariman, R. Subhash Reddy and Surya Kant,
Relevant Section:
Companies Act, 1956 - Section 433; Companies Act, 1956 - Section 434
Equivalent Citation:
2019(13)SCALE61, 2019(10)SCC750, AIR2019SC4758, 2019(6)ALD200, MANU/SC/1319/2019
Number of pages in the original judgement: 4
Case Note:

Insolvency - Winding up Petition - Maintainability of - Section 7 of Insolvency and Bankruptcy Code, 2016 - National Company Law Appellate Tribunal ("NCLAT") by an order dismissed appeal filed by Shri Jignesh Shah against admission order, agreeing with NCLT that transaction would fall within meaning of "financial debt" under Code, and that, bar of limitation would not be attracted as Winding up Petition was filed within three years of date on which Code came into force, viz., 1st December, 2016 - Whether Winding up Petition, on date that it was filed was barred by lapse of time.

Brief Facts:

Writ Petition have been filed by Shri Jignesh Shah and Smt. Pushpa Shah respectively, both of whom were shareholders of La-Fin Financial Services Pvt. Ltd. ("La-Fin") assailing order of National Company Law Tribunal, Mumbai Bench ("NCLT") admitting a winding up petition that was filed by IL & FS Financial Services Ltd. ("IL & FS") against La-Fin before High Court which was transferred to the NCLT and then heard as a Section 7 application under Insolvency and Bankruptcy Code, 2016. The National Company Law Appellate Tribunal ("NCLAT") by an order dismissed the appeal filed by Shri Jignesh Shah against the aforesaid admission order, agreeing with the NCLT that transaction would fall within the meaning of "financial debt" under the Code, and that the bar of limitation would not be attracted as the Winding up Petition was filed within three years of date on which the Code came into force, viz., 1st December, 2016. Learned Senior Advocate appearing on behalf of the Petitioners/Appellants has raised only the statutory bar of limitation against IL & FS. According to the learned Senior Advocate, after this Court's judgment in B.K. Educational Services Pvt. Ltd. v. Parag Gupta and Associates, it is clear that the Limitation Act, 1963 ("Limitation Act") would apply to all Section 7 applications that are filed under the Code and that the residuary Article, i.e., Article 137 of the Limitation Act would be attracted to the facts of this case. As the Winding up Petition that has been transferred to the NCLT was filed on 21st October, 2016, i.e., beyond the period of three years prescribed (as the cause of action had arisen in August, 2012), it is clear that a time-barred winding up petition filed under Section 433 of the Companies Act, 1956 would not suddenly get resuscitated into a Section 7 petition under the Code filed within time, by virtue of the transfer of such petition.

Held, while allowing the Appeal:

1. With the introduction of Section 238A into the Code, the provisions of the Limitation Act apply to applications made under the Code. Winding up petitions filed before the Code came into force are now converted into petitions filed under the Code. What has, therefore, to be decided is whether the Winding up Petition, on the date that it was filed, is barred by lapse of time. If such petition is found to be time-barred, then Section 238A of the Code will not give a new lease of life to such a time-barred petition. On the facts of this case, it is clear that as the Winding up Petition was filed beyond three years from August, 2012 which is when, even according to IL & FS, default in repayment had occurred, it is barred by time. [10]

2. A suit for recovery based upon a cause of action that is within limitation cannot in any manner impact the separate and independent remedy of a winding up proceeding. In law, when time begins to run, it can only be extended in the manner provided in the Limitation Act. For

example, an acknowledgement of liability under Section 18 of the Limitation Act would certainly extend the limitation period, but a suit for recovery, which is a separate and independent proceeding distinct from the remedy of winding up would, in no manner, impact the limitation within which the winding up proceeding is to be filed, by somehow keeping the debt alive for the purpose of the winding up proceeding. [19]

3. A reading of provisions would show that the starting point of the period of limitation is when the company is unable to pay its debts, and that Section 434 is a deeming provision which refers to three situations in which a Company shall be deemed to be "unable to pay its debts" under Section 433(e). In the first situation, if a demand is made by the creditor to whom the company is indebted in a sum exceeding one lakh then due, requiring the company to pay the sum so due, and the company has for three weeks thereafter "neglected to pay the sum", or to secure or compound for it to the reasonable satisfaction of the creditor. "Neglected to pay" would arise only on default to pay the sum due, which would clearly be a fixed date depending on the facts of each case. Equally in the second situation, if execution or other process is issued on a decree or order of any Court or Tribunal in favour of a creditor of the company, and is returned unsatisfied in whole or in part, default on the part of the debtor company occurs. This again is clearly a fixed date depending on the facts of each case. And in the third situation, it is necessary to prove to the "satisfaction of the Tribunal" that the company is unable to pay its debts. Here again, the trigger point is the date on which default is committed, on account of which the Company is unable to pay its debts. This again is a fixed date that can be proved on the facts of each case. Thus, Section 433(e) read with Section 434 of the Companies Act, 1956 would show that the trigger point for the purpose of limitation for filing of a winding up petition under Section 433(e) would be the date of default in payment of the debt in any of the three situations mentioned in Section 434. [22]

4. The Bombay High Court judgment referred to in paragraph 23 of the judgment above states the law on winding up petitions filed under Section 433(a) of the Companies Act, 1956 correctly. The primary test is set out in paragraph 1, which is that a winding up petition is not a legitimate means of seeking to enforce payment of a debt which is bona fide disputed by the Company. Absent such dispute, the petition may be admitted. Equally, where the debt is bona fide disputed, there cannot be 'neglect to pay' within the meaning of Section 434(1)(a) of the Companies Act, 1956 so

that the deeming provision then does not come into play. Also, the moment there is a bona fide dispute, the debt is then not 'due'. The High Court also correctly appreciates that whether the company is commercially solvent is one of the considerations in order to determine whether the company is able to pay its debts or not. [28]

5. Even on the facts of this case, the Winding up Petition alleges that the ultimatum to the Respondent company asserting that the Respondent company was legally obliged to purchase the requisite shares in accordance with the terms of the Letter of Undertaking was on 7th January, 2013. By this date at the very latest, the cause of action for filing a petition under Section 433(e) certainly arose. Also, the statutory notice given on 3rd November, 2015 does not refer to any facts as to the commercial insolvency of La-Fin. The statutory notice only refers to the suit proceedings and attachment by the EOW which had taken place long before in December 2013. [29]

6. In the Winding up Petition itself, what is referred to is the fall in the assets of La-Fin to being worth approximately INR 200 crores as of October, 2016, which again does not correlate with 3rd November, 2015, being the date on which the statutory notice was itself issued. This again is only for the purpose of appointing an Officer of the Court as Official Liquidator in order to manage the day-to-day affairs and otherwise secure and safeguard the assets of the Respondent company. There is no averment in the petition that thanks to these or other facts the Company's substratum has disappeared, or that the Company is otherwise commercially insolvent. It is clear therefore that even on facts, the company's substratum disappearing or the commercial insolvency of the company has not been pleaded. Whereas, in Form-1, upon transfer of the winding up proceedings to the NCLT, what is correctly stated is that the date of default is 19th August, 2012; making it clear that three-years from that date had long since elapsed when the Winding up Petition Under Section 433(e) was filed on 21st October, 2016. [30]

7. Present Court allows Civil Appeal and dispose of the Writ Petition by holding that, the Winding up Petition filed on 21st October, 2016 being beyond the period of three-years mentioned in Article 137 of the Limitation Act is time-barred, and cannot therefore be proceeded with any further. Accordingly, the impugned judgment of the NCLAT and the judgment of the NCLT is set

• 20 •

Reliance Asset Reconstruction Company Ltd. vs. Hotel Poonja International Pvt. Ltd., 2021

Hon'ble Judges/Coram:
Indira Banerjee and Sanjiv Khanna, JJ.
Relevant Section:
Companies Act, 1956 - Section 433; Companies Act, 1956 - Section 434
Equivalent Citation:
IV(2021)BC336(SC), (2021)7SCC352, MANU/SC/0568/2021
Number of pages in the original judgement:6
Case Note:
Insolvency - Corporate Insolvency Resolution Process (CIRP) - Section 7 of the Insolvency and Bankruptcy Code, 2016 (IBC) - Default in loan repayment - Proceedings initiated by Appellant (Asset recovery Company) - Appellant pursuant to agreement with Assignor Bank substituted it in proceedings of debt recovery - Appellant filed CIRP before NCLT - Petition dismissed by NCLT finding reasons to be unjust - Appeal before NCLAT dismissed, also on the grounds of limitation - Hence, the present appeal - Whether the recovery had become time barred and thus rightly dismissed by NCLAT?
Brief Facts:
Respondent (Corporate Debtor) granted credit/loan facilities by Assignor Bank alongwith Corporation Bank. Pursuant to an agreement concerned, the Assignor Bank assigned its dues from the Corporate Debtor

to the Appellant. By a paripassu agreement executed by and between the Assignor Bank, Corporation Bank, and the Corporate Debtor, a paripassu charge was created on the movable and immovable properties of the Corporate Debtor, in favour of the two banks. The Corporate Debtor failed to repay the loan obtained from the Assignor Bank. The Assignor Bank, therefore, declared the account of the Corporate Debtor as a "Non Performing Asset" (NPA). Bank initiated debt recovery process. Corporate Debtor made settlement but failed to pay the settlement amount. Assignor Bank filed execution for recovery of the decretal amount after deducting money already paid by the Corporate Debtor. After the execution of the agreement with the Assignor Bank, the Appellant was substituted as applicant in place of the Assignor Bank. Appellant filed a petition before the NCLT for initiation of Corporate Insolvency Resolution Process (CIRP). NCLT, dismissed the said petition holding that provisions of the IBC could not be invoked for recovery of outstanding dues, but could only be invoked to initiate CIRP for just reasons. Appeal against the said order dismissed vide judgment impugned. NCLAT also held proceedings to be barred by law.

Held, while dismissing the Appeal:

In its application Under Section 7 of the IBC, the Appellant has not shown that the debt due to the Appellant from the Corporate Debtor is not barred by limitation. The right to sue accrued on 1st April 1993 when the amount of the Corporate Debtor with the Assignor Bank was declared NPA. In Part IV of its application Under Section 7 of the IBC, the Appellant declared the date of default as 1st April, 1993. The claim is apparently barred by limitation. [23]

Under Section 18 of the Limitation Act, 1963, the acknowledgement of liability in writing, signed by a party in respect of any right or property claimed by such party within the prescribed period of limitation to file a suit and/or application, leads to computation of the period of limitation afresh, from the time when the acknowledgement is so signed.[24]

In this case, the Corporate Debtor has not signed any acknowledgement in writing after the settlement of 30th June 2001, on the basis of which, a Recovery Certificate was issued by the DRT on 27th March 2003. An arrangement between the Assignor Bank and the Appellant and the consequential substitution of the Appellant as party to the Execution/ Recovery proceedings in the DRT does not save limitation to initiate proceedings Under Section 7 of IBC. In any case, even the amended

Recovery Certificate, relied upon by the Appellant, is dated 13th December, 2012. The application Under Section 7 of the IBC was filed almost 6 years after issuance of the amended Recovery Certificate.[25]

In any case, there are pending proceedings in the DRT, in respect of the dues of the Corporate Debtor. The Appellant has been substituted in place of the Assignor Bank in the execution proceedings in the DRT. There is an amended Certificate issued by the DRT. Orders have, from time to time, been passed in the Execution Proceedings. The Appellant is not without remedy against the Corporate Debtor.[37]

There is no infirmity in the judgment and order of the NCLAT under appeal that calls for interference of this Court. The appeal is therefore, dismissed.[39]

CHAPTER NINE

V. Nagarajan vs. SKS Ispat and Power Ltd. and Ors., 2021

Hon'ble Judges/Coram:

Dr. D.Y. Chandrachud, Vikram Nath and B.V. Nagarathna, JJ.

Relevant Section:

Section 420(3) of the Companies Act 2013

Equivalent Citation:

2021(4)RCR(Civil)650, MANU/SC/0956/2021

Case Note:

Insolvency - Filing of Appeal - Limitation - Appeal dismissed barred by limitation - Section 61 of the Insolvency and Bankruptcy Code 2016 - Statutory time limit of thirty days expired - No application for condonation of delay filed - Condonation of extended delays up to fifteen days also elapsed - Whether impugned judgment dismissing appeal as time barred sustainable?

Brief Facts:

The present appeal from the judgment of the National Company Law Appellate Tribunal (NCLAT) that dismissed the appeal as barred by limitation. Appeal was filed against the National Company Law Tribunal (NCLT) order dismissing Appellant's miscellaneous application in a liquidation proceeding, seeking interim relief against the invocation of a bank guarantee by R10 against the Corporate Debtor.

Held, while dismissing the Appeal:

The IBC is a complete code in itself and over-rides any inconsistencies that may arise in the application of other laws. [15]

Owing to the special nature of the IBC, the aggrieved party is expected to exercise due diligence and apply for a certified copy upon pronouncement of the order it seeks to assail, in consonance with the requirements of Rule 22(2) of the NCLAT Rules. Section 12(2) of the Limitation Act allows for an exclusion of the time requisite for obtaining a copy of the decree or order appealed against. It is not open to a person aggrieved by an order under the IBC to await the receipt of a free certified copy Under Section 420(3) of the Companies Act 2013 read with Rule 50 of the NCLT and prevent limitation from running. Accepting such a construction will upset the timely framework of the IBC. The litigant has to file its appeal within thirty days, which can be extended up to a period of fifteen days, and no more, upon showing sufficient cause.[21]

The Appellant having failed to apply for a certified copy, rendered the appeal filed before the NCLAT as clearly barred by limitation.[22]

The Appellant has demonstrated no effort on his part to secure a certified copy of the said order and has relied on the date of the uploading of the order (12 March 2020) on the website. The period of limitation for filing an appeal Under Section 61(1) against the order of the NCLT dated 31 December 2019, expired on 30 January 2020 in view of the thirty-day period prescribed Under Section 61(2). Any scope for a condonation of delay expired on 14 February 2020, in view of the outer limit of fifteen days prescribed under the proviso to Section 61(2). The lockdown from 23 March 2020 on account of the COVID-19 pandemic and the suomotu order of this Court has had no impact on the rights of the Appellant to institute an appeal in this proceeding and the NCLAT has correctly dismissed the appeal on limitation. Accordingly, the present appeal Under Section 62 of the IBC stands dismissed.[23]

CHAPTER TEN

The Company Law Board vs. The Upper Doab Sugar Mills Ltd. and Ors., 1976

Hon'ble Judges/Coram:

A.C. Gupta, H.R. Khanna and Raja Jaswant Singh, JJ.

Relevant Section:

COMPANIES ACT, 1956 - Section 269; COMPANIES ACT, 1956 - Section 637A

Equivalent Citation:

AIR1977SC831, [1977]47CompCas173(SC), (1976)2CompLJ423(SC), (1977)2SCC198, [1977]2SCR503, 1977(9)UJ79, MANU/SC/0061/1976

Case Notes:

Company - approval - Section 637 of Companies Act, 1956 - respondent-company appointed its managing directors - respondent applied to Central Government for approval of appointment of managing directors - appellant-board acting on behalf of Government while granting approval inserted condition prescribing maximum ceiling of salary of managing directors - respondent challenged insertion of such condition in High Court - High Court decided in favour of respondent - appeal - whether insertion of condition beyond powers of appellant - Section 637 provides that board may grant approval subject to condition it deems fit - insertion of condition in present case appropriate and proper - insertion of condition legal exercise of powers of board conferred under Act - appeal dismissed.

Brief Facts:

The respondent company, Upper Doab Sugar Mills Ltd., is a public limited company governed by the provisions of the Companies Act, 1956 (hereinafter referred to as the Act). The company has its registered office at Shamli, district Muzaffarnagar (Uttar Pradesh). Its main business is manufacture of sugar from sugar cane. It also manufactures spirits, industrial alcohols and rum from molasses. From 1951 onwards a firm of managing agents managed the respondent company. Two of the partners of that firm were Shri Rajinder Lal and Shri Narinder Lal. The managing agency agreement of that firm was to expire on January 14, 1967. On October 4, 1966 the Board of Directors of the company resolved not to continue the managing agency of the said firm and decided to appoint two managing directors to conduct and manage the affairs of the company. Accordingly, on October 8, 1966 in exercise of the powers under Article 117 of the articles of association of the company the Board of Directors resolved to appoint Shri Rajinder Lal and Shri Narinder Lal as the two managing directors of the company. The salary of each of the managing directors was fixed at Rs. 5,000/- per month. In addition to that, each managing director was to get commission at the rate of 3 1/2 per cent of the net profits of the company during a financial year computed in the manner laid down in Section 309(5) of the Act. Besides that, other service benefits such as gratuity, provident fund, free medical treatment, transportation and free furnished residential accommodation were to be provided to each of the managing directors. The resolution of the Board of Directors was placed before the shareholders of the company in a general meeting. The shareholders approved the said resolution to appoint Shri Rajinder Lal and Shri Harinder Lal as managing directors on the terms set out in that resolution. An application was thereafter made under Section 269 of the Act to Company Law Board, appellant, for obtaining approval to the appointment of Shri Rajinder Lal and Shri Harinder Lal as managing directors. The powers of the Central Government, it may be stated, have been delegated to the appellant Board for exercising, inter alias, powers under Section 269 of the Act. The appellant Board after obtaining some additional information and after some further correspondence granted as per letter dated September, 28, 1967 approved to the appointment of Shri Rajinder Lal and Shri Narinder Lal as managing directors of the company. The said approval was granted subject to the various terms and included the following condition:

The total remuneration of each managing director by way of commission and salary shall not exceed Rs. 1,20,000 (Rupees one lakh twenty thousand) per annum.

Held while allowing the appeal,

The High Court, in our opinion, was in error in quashing the order of the Board. We accordingly accept the appeals, set aside the judgment of the High Court and dismiss the writ petitions. Looking to all the facts, we leave the parties to bear their own costs throughout.

CHAPTER ELEVEN

Madras Bar Association vs. Union of India (UOI) and Ors., 2015

Hon'ble Judges/Coram:

H.L. Dattu, C.J.I., A.K. Sikri, Arun Mishra, Rohinton Fali Nariman and Amitava Roy, JJ.

Relevant Sections:

COMPANIES ACT, 2013 - Section 412(2); COMPANIES ACT, 2013 - Section 411; COMPANIES ACT, 2013 - Section 409; COMPANIES ACT, 2013 - Section 408

Equivalent Citations:

2015VII AD (S.C.) 229, [2015]126CLA111(SC), [2015]190CompCas484(SC), (2015)3CompLJ1(SC), (2015)4MLJ184(SC), 2015(6)SCALE331, (2015)8SCC583, 2015 (6) SCJ 671, [2015]131SCL26(SC), MANU/SC/0610/2015

Case Notes:

Constitution - Setting up of Tribunal - Validity thereof - Section 10FR of Companies Act, 1956 and Companies Act, 2013 - Present petition alleging that Government did not incorporate changes in law regarding National Company Law Tribunal (NCLT) and National Company Law Appellate Tribunal (NCLAT) as per norms fixed by present Court previously - Whether creation of NCLT and NCLAT was unconstitutional - Held, creation of constitution of NCLAT had been specifically upheld in previous judgment - Provision pertaining to constitution of NCLAT i.e. Section 10FR of Act, 1956 was duly taken note of - Distinguishing features were spelled out between NCLT-NCLAT and National Tax Tribunal by Constitution Bench - NCLT would deal with question of law in given case coming before it and also, factual disputes/aspects - NCLAT would have to revisit factual as well as legal issues to examine validity of orders passed by NCLT - It was not unknown, rather common practice to provide one appellate forum wherever enactment was complete Code for providing judicial remedies - Providing one right to appeal before Appellate forum is well accepted norm which is perceived as a healthy tradition - Petition disposed of. [11],[15],[16] and[17]

Constitution - Validity of provision - Sections 409 and 411 of Companies Act, 2013 and Companies Act, 1956 - Present petition filed to challenge prescription of qualifications including term of their office and salary allowances of President and Members of NCLT and Chairman and Members of NCLAT - Whether provision relating technical Members of NCLT or NCLAT almost same which was inserted by way of amendment in Act, 1956, were unconstitutional - Held, members holding ranks of Secretaries or Additional Secretaries alone could be considered for appointment as Technical members - Section 409(3)(a) and (c) of Act, 2003 were invalid as these provisions suffered from same vice - Section 411(3) of Act, 2013 as worded, providing for qualifications of technical Members, was also held to be invalid - For appointment of technical Members to NCLT, directions contained in previous judgment of Constitution Bench of present Court would have to be scrupulously followed - These corrections were required to be made in Section 409(3) of Act, 2013 to set right defects contained therein - Petition disposed of. [21] and[24]

Constitution - Selection Committee - Structure thereof - Section 425 of Companies Act, 2013 - Present petition filed challenging structure of Selection Committee for appointment of President and Members of NCLT and Chairperson and Members of NCLAT - Whether constitution of Selection Committee for selecting Members of NCLT and NCLAT was sustainable - Held, issue stood concluded by previous judgment, now binding precedent and bound Respondent equally - As per such judgment, selection committee would be composed of four members instead of five - Provisions of Section 412(2) of Act, 2013 were not valid and direction was issued to remove defect by bringing this provision in accord with previous judgment - Petitioner failed to prove that provisions were unconstitutional - Respondents were directed to take remedial measures as per directions contained in previous judgment - Petition disposed of. [26],[28],[29] and[33]

Brief Facts:

Writ petition, in this behalf, was filed by the Petitioner in the High Court of Madras which culminated into the judgment dated 30.03.2004. The High Court held that creation of NCLT and vesting the powers hitherto exercised by the High Court and the Company Law Board ('CLB' for short) in the said Tribunal was not unconstitutional. However, at the same time, the High Court pointed out certain defects in various provisions of Part 1B and Part 1C of the Act, 1956 and, in particular, in Sections 10FD(3)(f)(g)(h), 10FE, 10FF, 10FL(2), 10FR(3), 10FT. Declaring that those provisions as existed offended the basic Constitutional scheme of separation of powers, it was held that unless these provisions are appropriately amended by removing the defects which were also specifically spelled out, it would be unconstitutional to constitute NCLT and NCLAT to exercise the jurisdiction which is being exercised by the High Court or the CLB. The Petitioner felt aggrieved by that part of the judgment vide which establishments of NCLT and NCLAT was held to be Constitutional. On the other hand, Union of India felt dissatisfied with the other part of the judgment whereby aforesaid provisions contained in Parts 1B and 1C of the Act, 1956 were perceived as suffering from various legal and Constitutional infirmities. Thus, both Union of India as well as the Petitioner filed appeals against that judgment of the Madras High Court. Those appeals were decided by the Constitution Bench, as mentioned above.

Held while disposing off the appeal,

Before we part, we must mention that the affidavit dated 07.05.2015 is filed on behalf of the Respondents mentioning therein the steps that have been taken till date towards setting up of NCLT and NCLAT. It is pointed out that the approval for creation of one post of Chairperson and five posts of Members of NCLAT as well as one post of President and 62 posts of Members of NCLT and two posts of Registrar one each for NCLT and NCLAT and one post of Secretary, NCLT was obtained and the approval was also obtained for creation of 246 posts of supporting staff of NCLT and NCLAT. It is also mentioned that following draft Rules have already been prepared in consultation with the Legislative Department, Ministry of Law: (i) NCLAT (Salaries, Allowances and other terms and conditions of service of the Chairperson and other Members) Rules, 2014, (ii) NCLT (Salary, Allowances and other Terms and Conditions of Service of President and other Members) Rules, 2013. Draft Recruitment Rules for the supporting staff were also prepared in consultation with Legislative Department, Ministry of Law. It is further mentioned that draft Rules with regard to manner of functioning of NCLT/NCLAT etc. were prepared in order to place them before the Chairperson/President of NCLAT/NCLT on their appointment for finalization as per the provisions of the Companies Act, 2013. These Rules cover provisions with regard to manner of functioning of NCLT/NCLAT; manner in which applications for various approvals shall be made by applicants and approved; and specific procedural requirements with regard to applications/matters relating to compromises/ arrangements/amalgamations; prevention of oppression and mismanagement; revival and rehabilitation of sick companies; winding up and other miscellaneous requirements. Space for Principal Bench and other Benches of NCLT, including a special Bench at Delhi to deal with transferred cases of BIFR and AAIFR had also been identified. Process initiated for renting space in some locations, which was discontinued in view of the pending petition, can be restarted at a short notice. Budget heads have been created for meeting the expenditure for NCLT and NCLAT. Allocated funds for 2014-2015 had to be surrendered in view of the delay in settling up the Tribunals.

32. From the aforesaid, it seems the only step which is left to make NCLT and NCLAT functional is to appoint President and Members of NCLT and Chairperson and Members of NCLAT.

33. Since, the functioning of NCLT and NCLAT has not started so far and its high time that these Tribunals start functioning now, we hope that the Respondents shall take remedial measures as per the directions contained in this judgment at the earliest, so that the NCLT & NCLAT are adequately manned and start functioning in near future.

34. Writ petition stands disposed of in the aforesaid manner.

CHAPTER TWELVE

Integrated Finance Company Ltd. vs. Reserve Bank of India and Ors., 2013

Hon'ble Judges/Coram:

S.S. Nijjar and Pinaki Chandra Ghose, JJ.

Relevant Sections:

Companies Act, 1956 - Section 235, Section 236, Section 237, Section 238, Section 239, Section 240, Section 241, Section 242, Section 243, Section 244, Section 245, Section 246, Section 247, Section 248, Section 249, Section 250, Section 251, Section 288, Section 32, Section 391, Section 392, Section 393, Section 394, Section 391(1), Companies Act, 1956 - Section 391(1)(a), Section 391(2), Section 393(1), Section 393(1)(a), Section 402, Section 58A

Equivalent Citation:

2013IX AD (S.C.) 606, IV(2013)BC16, [2013]115CLA329(SC), [2013]179CompCas390(SC), (2013)4CompLJ1(SC), (2013)4CompLJ1(SC), ILR2013(3)Kerala283, JT2013(10)SC283, 2013-4-LW293, 2013(9)SCALE600, (2015)13SCC772, [2013]121SCL94(SC), MANU/SC/0710/2013

Case Note:

Companies Act, 1956- Section 391--Though, whilst considering a compromise scheme submitted for approval, the Company Court is not required to examine the scheme meticulously like an accountant, the Court is not bound to superficially add its seal of approval to the scheme merely because it had received the approval of the requisite majority at the meeting held for that purpose--Court has to ensure that the scheme is not a camouflage for a purpose other than the ostensible reasons.

Brief Facts:

The appellant, a Non-Banking Finance Company, filed the appeal, being aggrieved by the Judgment of a Division Bench of the Madras High Court. The proceedings originated with the appellant filing a scheme of compromise with it creditors before the Madras High Court, under Section 391, seeking approval of the Company Court. The circumstances which lead the appellant to file the compromise scheme was that the Reserve Bank of India had found out certain violations in the functioning of the Company and in exercise of its powers under Section 45MB(1) of the Reserve Bank of India Act, issued a circular to the appellant Company prohibiting it from accepting deposits from any person, in any form, whether by way of fresh deposits or renewal of the existing deposits or otherwise, until further orders. The learned Judge before whom the scheme was submitted permitted the company to convene a meeting of its deposit holders, for approval of its scheme. The meeting was held and the scheme approved by majority. Thereafter the appellant preferred a petition before the High Court under Section 391(2) of the Companies Act, seeking sanction for the scheme of compromise. The prayer for approval was opposed by the Reserve Bank of India as well as the Depositors Association. The objections were overruled by the learned Single Judge and the scheme was approved. This decision was challenged in appeal before the Division Bench by the Reserve Bank of India as well as the Depositors Association, mainly contending that in view of the non obstante clause containing Section 45QA of the Reserve Bank of India Act. Chapter IIIB will prevail over the provisions of the Companies Act. It was also contended that the appellant was guilty of nondisclosure of the RBTs direction. Accepting the contentions, the Division Bench declined to approve the scheme and set aside the order passed by the Company Court. Assailing the Judgment of the Division Bench it was contended on behalf of the appellant that the RBI Act and the Companies Act must be read in their own spheres, since both operate in altogether different fields and therefore the application of Sections 391 to 394 of the Companies Act is not in any way affected by Section 45QA of the Reserve Bank of India Act. This contention was countered by the Reserve Bank stating that Section 45QA(1) require that every deposit accepted by an NBFC, unless renewed, shall be repaid in accordance with the terms and conditions of such deposit, which guarantee cannot be overcome by getting the scheme containing contrary provisions approved by the Company Court. The Apex Court after a detailed consideration of the relevant provisions as well as precedents dismissed the appeal holding that Sections 45QA of the Reserve Bank of India Act has overriding effect over Section 391 of the Companies Act and hence a scheme containing provisions contrary to the mandate of Section 45QA cannot be approved. Dismissing the Appeal;

Held while dismissing the appeal:

Chapter IIIB of the RBI has been incorporated through RBI (Amendment) Ordinance, 1997, subsequently replaced by the RBI (Amendment) Act, 1997. The Statement of Objects and Reasons make it abundantly clear that before the amendment, the unincorporated bodies circumvented the statutory restrictions by floating different partnership firms as and when a firm reached the level of 250 depositors. It was also reiterated that several unincorporated bodies were advertising aggressively through various media, soliciting deposits from public by offering high rates of interest and other incentives. The Amendment Act provides several safeguards for NBFCs so as to ensure their viability. This includes compulsory' registration of NBFCs with RBI, stipulation of minimum need in the funds requirements, creation of reserved funds and transfer of certain percentage of profits every year to the fund; and prescription of liquidity requirements. The RBI has also been vested with powers to issue guidelines intended to ensure sound and healthy operations and the quality of assets of these companies. The RBI was also empowered to issue directions to Auditors of NBFCs to order special Audits in NBFCs, prohibited acceptance of deposits by NBFCs and make applications for winding up of NBFCs. It is specifically noticed that earlier the only recourse available to the depositors was to approach the Court of Law for redressal of grievances. However by the Amendment, powers have been vested with the Company Law-Board for directing the defaulter NBFCs to make repayment for the deposit interest with a view to protect the interest of depositors. The NBFCs have been totally prohibited from accepting deposits for the purpose other than for personal use, if unincorporated. They have been permitted to continue to take deposit after incorporating themselves within the regulatory framework. The unincorporated bodies have also been specifically prohibited for issuing any advertisements in any form. The real intent is set out in Paragraph 6, which is as under:

"6. There are reports of several finance companies and incorporated bodies having failed to repay the deposits collected from unsuspecting depositors who have been tempted by the attractive returns and incentives offered. Concern has been expressed in several quarters on the need to take urgent steps to regulate the activities of such companies and unincorporated bodies."

Keeping in view the aforesaid objects and reasons, it becomes evident that Chapter IIIB of the RBI Act is a self contained code. It is not possible for us to accept the submissions of the learned counsel for the appellants that the RBI Act and the Companies Act operate in distinct and different fields. We are unable to accept the submission of the learned counsel for the appellants that the provision contained in the RBI Act being regulatory in nature will not apply to cases of schemes submitted for approval under the Companies Act. Even applying the ratio of the judgments cited by the learned senior counsel, there is no justification for lessening the scope of the applicability of the non obstante clause in Section 45Q of the RBI Act. It states in categoric terms that provisions of Chapter IIIB shall have effect notwithstanding anything inconsistent therewith contained in any other law. The overriding effect extends not only to any other law for the time-being in force but also to any instrument having effect by virtue of having such law. The reasons for giving such categoric overriding effect are evident from the objects and reasons given in the Amendment Act. The magnitude of the exploitation of the poor sections of the society, leading to utter destruction of innumerable families was the underlying impetus to bring the NBFCs under strict control. Therefore, we have no hesitation in concluding that Chapter III B of the RBI Act is a complete code in itself. The Companies Act is a prior enactment as the same was enacted in the year 1956, whereas, Chapter IIIB was inserted in the RBI Act (55 of 1963) w.e.f. 1964. Section 45QA was inserted by the Act No. 23 of 1997 w.e.f. 9th January, 1997. Thus, provisions of the RBI Act would prevail over the Companies Act, it being a later enactment. It is a settled proposition of law that a later enactment will override the earlier enactment. In our opinion, Chapter IIIB has been given an overriding effect over all other laws including Companies Act by incorporating Section 45Q with a clear intention to ensure that in a case of NBFC, a scheme under Section 391 of the Companies Act cannot be entertained unless it is in conformity with the provisions of Section 45QA of the RBI Act.

CHAPTER THIRTEEN

Surendra Trading Company vs. Juggilal Kamlapat Jute Mills Company Ltd. and Ors., 2017

Hon'ble Judges/Coram:

A.K. Sikri and Ashok Bhushan, JJ.

Equivalent Citation:

2018(2)ABR324, AIR2018SC186, 2018(1) AKR 663, 2018(4)ALLMR462, [2017]141CLA174(SC), [2017]205CompCas119(SC), (2018)1CompLJ217(SC), 2018-1-LW813, (2017)16SCC143, 2019 (1) SCJ 641, [2017]144SCL198(SC), MANU/SC/1248/2017

Relevant Section:

SECTION 397 and 398 of Companies Act, 1956

Case Note:

Company - Removal of defects - Expiry of time - Sections 7(5),9(5) and 10(4) of Insolvency and Bankruptcy Code, 2016 - National Company Law Appellate Tribunal held that time of seven days prescribed in proviso to Sub-section (5) of Section 9 of Code was mandatory in nature and if defects contained in application filed by operational creditor for initiating corporate insolvency resolution against corporate debtor were not removed within seven days of receipt of notice given by adjudicating authority for removal of such objections, then such application filed under Section 9 of Code was liable to be rejected - Hence, present appeal - Whether provision of removing defects within seven days was mandatory in nature.

Brief Facts:

The National Company Law Appellate Tribunal was held that the time of seven days prescribed in proviso to Sub-section (5) of Section 9 of the

Insolvency and Bankruptcy Code, 2016 was mandatory in nature and if the defects contained in the application filed by the operational creditor for initiating corporate insolvency resolution against a corporate debtor were not removed within seven days of the receipt of notice given by the adjudicating authority for removal of such objections, then such an application filed under Section 9 of the Code was liable to be rejected.

Held, while allowing the appeal:

(i) This Court was not able to decipher any valid reason given while coming to the conclusion that the period mentioned in proviso was mandatory. The order of the NCLAT, proceeds to take note of the provisions of Section 12 of the Code and points out the time limit for completion of insolvency resolution process was one hundred eighty days, which period could be extended by another ninety days However, that could hardly provide any justification to construe the provisions of proviso to Sub-section (5) of Section 9 in the manner in which it was done. It was to be borne in mind that limit of one hundred eighty days mentioned in Section 12 also starts from the date of admission of the application. Period prior thereto which was consumed, after the filing of the application under Section 9, whether by the Registry of the adjudicating authority in scrutinising the application or by the applicant in removing the defects or by the adjudicating authority in admitting the application is not to be taken into account. In fact, till the objections were removed it is not to be treated as application validly filed inasmuch as only after the application was complete in every respect it was required to be entertained. In this scenario, making the period of seven days contained in the proviso as mandatory did not commend to this Court. No purpose was going to be served by treating this period as mandatory. In a given case there may be weighty, valid and justifiable reasons for not able to remove the defects within seven days. Notwithstanding the same, the effect would be to reject the application. [20]

(ii) The moot question would be as to whether such a rejection would be treated as rejecting the application on merits thereby debarring the application from filing fresh application or it is to be treated as an administrative order since the rejection was because of the reason that defects were not removed and application was not examined on merits. In the former case it would be travesty of justice that even if the case of the applicant on merits is very strong, the applicant was shown the door without adjudication of his application on merits. If the latter alternative was accepted, then rejection of the application in the first instance was not going to serve any purpose as the applicant would be permitted to file fresh application, complete in all aspects, which would have to be entertained. Thus, in either case, no purpose was served by treating the said provision as mandatory. [21]

(iii) The judgments cited by the NCLAT and the principle contained therein applied while deciding that period of fourteen days within which the adjudicating authority had to pass the order is not mandatory but directory in nature would equally apply while interpreting proviso to Sub-section (5) of Section 7, Section 9 or Sub-section (4) of Section 10 as well. After all, the applicant did not gain anything by not removing the objections inasmuch as till the objections were removed, such an application would not be entertained. Therefore, it was in the interest of the applicant to remove the defects as early as possible. [23]

(iv) Therefore, part of the impugned judgment of NCLAT which holds proviso to Sub-section (5) of Section 7 or proviso to Sub-section (5) of Section 9 or proviso to Sub-section (4) of Section 10 to remove the defects within seven days as mandatory and on failure applications to be rejected, was set aside. [26]

CHAPTER FOURTEEN

Ghanshyam Sarda vs. Shiv Shankar Trading Company 2014

Hon'ble Judges/Coram:

Anil R. Dave and U.U. Lalit, JJ.

Relevant Section:

Companies Act, 1956 - Section 22(1), Section- 26 and Section - 32(1) , Sick Industrial Companies (Special Provisions) Act, 1985 [Repealed] - Section 16; Sick Industrial Companies (Special Provisions) Act, 1985 [Repealed] - Section 17(1); Sick Industrial Companies (Special Provisions) Act, 1985 [Repealed] - Section 22(1)

Equivalent Citation:

2015VII AD (S.C.) 525, AIR2015SC403, 2015(1)ALLMR421, 4(2014)BC711(SC), 2014 (4) CCC 225 , 2015(4) CHN (SC) 99, [2014]123CLA445(SC), [2015]188CompCas268(SC), (2015)1CompLJ565(SC), 2015(4)MhLJ157(SC), (2015)1MLJ497, 2015MPLJ34(SC), 2014(12)SCALE732, (2014)1SCC298, (2015)1SCC298, 2014 (10) SCJ 271, 2015(2)SCT24(SC), MANU/SC/1029/2014

Case Note:

SICA - Determination of control - Positive net worth - Sections 22(1), 26 and 32(1) of Sick Industrial Companies (Special Provisions) Act, 1985 - Appellant filed petition against order of injunction restraining Board of Industrial and Financial Reconstruction (BIFR) from proceeding further - High Court disposed of petition on ground that since all proceedings before BIFR stood stayed, further proceeding would be of no legal consequence - Hence, present appeal - Whether BIFR would lose control over sick company even if it had revived on its own and its net worth had become positive - Held, Act gave complete supervisory control to BIFR over affairs of sick Industrial Company from stage of registration of reference and questions concerning status of sickness of such company were in exclusive domain of BIFR - Any submission by anyone including Company that by certain developments Company's net worth had become positive, no such scheme for revival needed to be undertaken, could only be dealt with by BIFR - Aspects of revival of such company being completely within its exclusive domain, it was BIFR alone, which could determine issue whether such company now stood revived or not - Jurisdiction of Civil Court in respect of these matters stood completely excluded - BIFR alone was empowered to determine whether net worth had become positive as result of which it would cease to had such jurisdiction - Further, BIFR was considering Draft Rehabilitation Scheme which was stage under Section 18(3) of Act and was completely covered by period under Section 22 of Act - Suit as framed for recovery of money filed without consent of BIFR was not competent and maintainable - Impugned order set aside - Appeal allowed. [paras 27, 28 and 29]

Brief Facts:

A company named J.K. Jute Mill Company Ltd. (hereinafter referred to as 'the company') having its registered office at Kanpur, Uttar Pradesh filed Reference No. 149 of 1994 before the Board for Industrial and Financial Reconstruction ("BIFR" for short) under the provisions of the Act. Though the scheme was initially sanctioned for reconstruction, the BIFR subsequently held the scheme to have failed and directed the company to be wound up. These orders were stayed by the Appellate Authority for Industrial and Financial Reconstruction ("AAIFR" for short) and further proceedings before the BIFR continued. While the matter was thus pending, "Sarda Group" took over the Company through Rainey Park Suppliers Private Ltd. (RPSPL) in 2007. BIFR by its order dated 17.12.2008 approved such take over of the management. The management of the company was handed over to Shri Govind Sarda. It appears that in 2009, Shri Govind Sarda assigned the debt held by RPSPL in favour of an entity named Libra Retailer Pvt. Ltd. (LRPL) and he is stated to have handed over Jute Mill of the company to a third party. As he failed to revive the company, show cause notice for winding up was issued by the BIFR. This action was challenged by the Company by filing Appeal No. 186 of 2009 before the AAIFR which appeal is still pending.

4. At this stage, Shri Ghanshyam Sarda, (hereinafter referred to as the present Appellant) filed an application for impleading himself in the proceedings which application was accepted by AAIFR. Upon this order being challenged, the High Court of Delhi in W.P. No. 2839 of 2010 held the present Appellant to be entitled to present his point of view in the form of proposal/scheme, which order was confirmed by this Court by dismissing Special Leave Petition filed at the instance of the Company. In terms of the aforesaid orders the BIFR impleaded the present Appellant who thereafter submitted a proposal for revival of the company and also filed MA No. 162 of 2012 in the BIFR for restoration of shareholding pattern. On 18.02.2013 the BIFR issued directions to the operating agency to consider the scheme of the present management and the scheme submitted by the present Appellant and thereafter submit a fully tied up Draft Revival Scheme ("DRS" for short). The BIFR fixed the next date for hearing of MA 162 of 2012 on 04.04.2013. In the proceedings dated 27.02.2013, it was decided that the DRS be circulated seeking objections and suggestions from all the concerned.

Held while allowing the appeal,

In the circumstances, we allow the present appeals and set aside the order dated 06.01.2014 passed by the High Court of Gauhati in FAO No. 10 of 2013 and Writ Petition Nos. 4303 of 2013 and 6286 of 2013. It is held that the Title Suit No. 166 of 2013 pending on the file of the learned Civil Court at Kamrup, Gauhati is not maintainable insofar as it seeks declaration that the company was no longer a sick company within the meaning of the Act and that the BIFR ceased to have jurisdiction over the company and that all the proceedings in the BIFR after filing of the positive balance-sheet were without jurisdiction. Consequently the order of injunction passed by the Civil Court is set aside. Insofar as the said Suit pertains to the claim for recovery of money from the Company, the Suit could lie and be proceeded with only after express consent of the BIFR is received by the Plaintiff. We direct that the company i.e., J.K. Jute Mills Company Ltd. having its registered office at Kanpur U.P. continues to be under the jurisdiction of the BIFR. We leave it to the BIFR to satisfy itself and determine the issues whether the net worth of the company has turned positive or not. If the BIFR is so satisfied, it shall de-register the company and upon such declaration the company will be out of the supervisory jurisdiction of the BIFR under the Act. Needless to say that if the BIFR is not satisfied that the net worth of the company has turned positive, it shall go ahead and consider the scheme for revival of the company. We direct the BIFR to complete this exercise within two months from date of receipt of this order. We have refrained from dealing with the matter concerning the merits or de-merits of the claim that the net worth has turned positive nor have we dealt with the report made by the State Bank of India in its Special Investigative Audit. We leave these issues to be considered by the BIFR at an appropriate stage. We have also not dealt with the submissions alleging bias as the matters in that behalf are still pending consideration before the authorities and we leave these issues to be dealt with at an appropriate stage.

32. Since in our view the company continues to be a sick company and it was not competent for anyone except the BIFR to determine whether the net worth of the company had turned positive, we hold the sale of Katihar property effected by the company without express leave or permission of the BIFR to be questionable. However, since the transferee of that property is not before this Court we relegate this matter for appropriate assessment by the BIFR after issuing due notice to the transferee. We also leave it to the BIFR to consider and assess whether there was any necessity or expediency to sell the property in question. If in its opinion such expediency and necessity are established, the BIFR may also consider whether the value that the property has fetched is adequate or not. If the value is adequate it may confirm the sale in favour of the transferee. However, if the value in its opinion is inadequate, it shall give offer and adequate time to the transferee to make good the deficit. In any case if the sale is held to be bad or if the transferee is not willing to make good the deficit, the entire consideration for the transaction be returned to the transferee. In such eventuality whatever the transferee has paid in excess of the consideration money towards stamp duty and registration shall be recovered from the Directors and persons responsible for effecting such sale on behalf of the company.

33. Now we turn to the filing of the civil suit in the instant case and its conduct. The original Plaintiff had sought consent of the BIFR Under Section 22(1) of the Act and was before the BIFR on 04.04.2013. However, he did not disclose either the factum that he had so sought such consent or that the BIFR was in seisin of the matter and considering whether the net worth of the company had turned positive. Non-disclosure of these two essential facts, in our view, was not accidental. We therefore impose costs of Rs. 5 lacs on the original Plaintiff which shall be deposited within three months from the date of this order, failing which action in contempt shall

be initiated against the original Plaintiff. The costs shall be deposited to the account of the Supreme Court Legal Services Authority. Though the conduct of the company as Defendant before the Civil Court was of the same order, since it is a sick company we refrain from imposing any costs on the company. No other order as to costs.

34. The appeals are allowed in the aforesaid terms. FAO No. 10 of 2013 thus stands allowed and Writ Petition Nos. 4303 of 2013 and 6286 of 2013 are dismissed. As regards Contempt Petition Nos. 338 and 375 of 2014, since this Court had not issued any notice to the alleged contemnors, we have not dealt with said petitions. By a separate order we issue appropriate notice to the alleged contemnors.

CHAPTER FIFTEEN

Ebix Singapore Private Limited and Ors. vs. Committee of Creditors of Educomp Solutions Limited and Ors., 2021

Hon'ble Judges/Coram:

Dr. D.Y. Chandrachud and M.R. Shah, JJ.

Relevant Section:

Companies (Amendment) Act, 2017 - Section 10, Companies (Amendment) Act, 2017 - Section 3AA, Companies (Amendment) Act, 2017 - Section 3AB, Companies (Amendment) Act, 2017 - Section 210; Companies Act, 2013 - Section 213

Citation:

MANU/SC/0628/2021

Case Note:

Insolvency - Withdrawal of Resolution Plan - Validity - Sections 60(5), 61 of the Insolvency and Bankruptcy Code, 2016 (IBC) - Impugned judgment set aside withdrawalof Resolution holding it being barred by res judicata and lack of jurisdiction - Whether impugned findings sustainable?

Brief Facts:

The present set of appeals raised the issue as to whether resolution plan once resolution plan submitted can be withdrawn? In the instant appeals, Court took the issue in the background that IBC does not provide any such provision and once it is so, should Court permit withdrawals.

Held, while disposing the Appeals:

Judicial restraint must not only be exercised while adjudicating upon the constitutionality of the statute relating to economic policy but also in matters of interpretation of economic statutes, where the interpretative maneuvers of the Court have an effect of transgressing into the law-making power of the legislature and disturbing the delicate balance of separation of powers between the legislature and the judiciary. In this case, if Resolution Applicants are permitted to seek modifications after subsequent negotiations or a withdrawal after a submission of a Resolution Plan to the Adjudicating Authority as a matter of law, it would dictate the commercial wisdom and bargaining strategies of all prospective Resolution Applicants who are seeking to participate in the process and the successful Resolution Applicants who may wish to negotiate a better deal, owing to myriad factors that are peculiar to their own case. [146]

The IBC is silent on whether a successful Resolution Applicant can withdraw its Resolution Plan. However, the statutory framework laid down under the IBC and the CIRP Regulations provide a step-by-step procedure which is to be followed from the initiation of CIRP to the approval by the Adjudicating Authority. Even a modification to the RFRP is envisaged by the CIRP Rules and is subject to a timeline. The absence of any exit routes being stipulated under the statute for a successful Resolution Applicant is indicative of the IBC's proscription of any attempts at withdrawal at its behest. [147]

This Court is cognizant that the extraordinary circumstance of the COVID-19 pandemic would have had a significant impact on the businesses of Corporate Debtors and upon successful Resolution Applicants whose Plans may not have been sanctioned by the Adjudicating Authority in time, for myriad reasons. But the legislative intent of the statute cannot be overridden by the Court to render outcomes that can have grave economic implications which will impact the viability of the IBC.[201]

The residual powers of the Adjudicating Authority under the IBC cannot be exercised to create procedural remedies which have substantive outcomes on the process of insolvency. Enabling withdrawals or modifications of the Resolution Plan at the behest of the successful Resolution Applicant, once it has been submitted to the Adjudicating Authority after due compliance with the procedural requirements and timelines, would create another tier of negotiations which will be wholly unregulated by the statute.[202]

The NCLT and the NCLAT should endeavor, on a best effort basis, to strictly adhere to the timelines stipulated under the IBC and clear pending resolution plans forthwith. Judicial delay was one of the major reasons for the failure of the insolvency regime that was in effect prior to the IBC.[205]

Appeals preferred by Ebix (Civil Appeal 3224 of 2020) and Seroco (Civil Appeal 295 of 2021) stand dismissed. The parties to the appeal preferred by Kundan Care (Civil Appeal 3560 of 2020) shall abide by the directions issued by this Court in exercise of its Article 142 powers as a one-time relief.

National Company Law Tribunal and Appellate Tribunal Bar Association vs. Ministry of Corporate Affairs and Ors., 2021

Hon'ble Judges/Coram:

L. Nageswara Rao, Hemant Gupta and S. Ravindra Bhat, JJ.

Relevant Section:

Companies Act, 2013 - Section 413

Equivalent Citation:

(2021)3CompLJ78(SC), [2021]167SCL238(SC), MANU/SC/0618/2021

Brief Facts:

The National Company Law Tribunal and Appellate Tribunal Bar Association has filed this writ petition seeking a direction to the Respondent to fill up the vacancies of Chairman, NCLAT and President of NCLT without any further delay. A further direction was sought to issue letters of appointment to the candidates pursuant to the selection procedure initiated in 2019 and to fill up the remaining vacancies of Members of NCLT and NCLAT. The Petitioner has also sought a direction to extend the term of six Members of the NCLT and NCLAT for a further period of five years as they are completing the tenure by June, 2021.

Held while disposing off the appeal,

As the Government has already initiated the process of reappointment by writing to the Hon'ble Chief Justice, we trust and hope that the reappointment process should be completed expeditiously, as there is no necessity of issuance of any advertisement for participation of other eligible candidates. Reappointment of members can be considered separately without waiting for the process of fresh appointments to commence. As the strength of the members of the NCLT and NCLAT is depleting which would be detrimental to the smooth functioning of the Tribunals, we direct the Government to complete the process at the earliest and not later than two months.

6. Writ petition and pending applications, if any, shall stand disposed of.

CHAPTER SEVENTEEN

K. Kishan vs. Vijay Nirman Company Pvt. Ltd., 2018

Hon'ble Judges/Coram:
Rohinton Fali Nariman and Indu Malhotra, JJ.

Equivalent Citation:
2019(193)AIC88, I(2019)BC3(SC), 2018(5)BomCR705, 2019(4) CHN (SC) 10, [2018]146CLA1(SC), (2018)4CompLJ168(SC), 2019(1)CTC484, 2018(II)CLR(SC)664, (2018)8MLJ177, 2018(4)RCR(Civil)197, 2018(10)SCALE256, [2018]150SCL110(SC), MANU/SC/0872/2018

Relevant Sections:
397 AND 398 OF COMPANIES ACT, 1956

Case Notes:

Arbitration - Operational debt - Pending of award - Section 34 of Arbitration and Conciliation Act, 1996 - Disputes arose between parties in respect to contract entered between parties and same were referred to Arbitral Tribunal, which delivered its Award - Petition under Section 34 of Act was filed for setting aside of award - Thereafter petition was filed under Section 9 of Insolvency and Bankruptcy Code, 2016 to Company Law Tribunal who held that fact that Section 34 petition was pending was irrelevant for reason that claim stood admitted, and there was no stay of Award - On appeal, Appellate Tribunal confirmed order passed by Tribunal - Hence, present appeal - Whether Insolvency and Bankruptcy Code, 2016 could be invoked in respect of operational debt where Arbitral Award had been passed against operational debtor, which had not yet been finally adjudicated upon.

Brief Facts:

The disputes and differences arose between the parties in respect to contract entered between parties and the same were referred to an Arbitral

Tribunal, which delivered its Award. Section 34 petition was filed under the Arbitration and Conciliation Act, 1996 challenging the said Award. Thereafter that a petition was filed under Section 9 of the Code to National Company Law Tribunal who held that fact that a Section 34 petition was pending was irrelevant for the reason that the claim stood admitted, and there was no stay of the Award. On appeal, the Appellate Tribunal held that since Form V of Part 5 of the Insolvency & Bankruptcy Rules, 2016 requires particulars of an order of an arbitral panel adjudicating on the default, this would have to be treated as a record of an operational debt, as a result of which the petition would have to be admitted, as was correctly done by the Tribunal.

Held, while allowing the appeal:

(i) It was clear that operational creditors could not use the Insolvency Code either prematurely or for extraneous considerations or as a substitute for debt enforcement procedures. The alarming result of an operational debt contained in an arbitral award for a small amount of say, two lakhs of rupees, could not possibly jeopardize an otherwise solvent company worth several crores of rupees. Such a company would be well within its rights to state that it is challenging the Arbitral Award passed against it, and the mere factum of challenge would be sufficient to state that it disputes the Award. Such a case would clearly come within case of Mobilox Innovations, being a case of a pre-existing ongoing dispute between the parties. The Code could not be used in terrorem to extract this sum of money of two lakhs rupees even though it may not be finally payable as adjudication proceedings in respect thereto were still pending. The object of the Code, at least insofar as operational creditors are concerned, was to put the insolvency process against a corporate debtor only in clear cases where a real dispute between the parties as to the debt owed did not exist. [13]

(ii) It may hasten to add that there may be cases where a Section 34 petition challenging an Arbitral Award may clearly and unequivocally be barred by limitation, in that it can be demonstrated to the Court that the period of ninety days plus the discretionary period of thirty days had clearly expired, after which either no petition Under Section 34 of Act had been filed or a belated petition under Section 34 of Act had been filed. It was only in such clear cases that the insolvency process may then be put into operation. [19]

(iii) The Appellate Tribunal was in error in referring to Section 238 of the Code. Section 238 of the Code would apply in case there is an inconsistency between the Code and the Arbitration Act in the present case. On the contrary, the Award passed under the Arbitration Act together with the steps taken for its challenge would only make it clear that the operational debt, in the present case, happen to be a disputed one. [22]

CHAPTER EIGHTEEN

63 Moons Technologies Ltd. and Ors. vs. Union of India (UOI) and Ors., 2019

Hon'ble Judges/Coram:

Rohinton Fali Nariman and Vineet Saran, JJ.

Equivalent Citation: [2019]150CLA209(SC), [2019]217CompCas181(SC), (2020)1CompLJ229(SC), 2019(7)SCALE50, (2019)18SCC401, MANU/SC/0629/2019

Relevant Section:

Companies Act, 1956 - Section 396

Case Note:

Company - Amalgamation order - Challenge thereto -Articles 19, 14 and Article 31A of Constitution of India, 1950 and Section 396 of Companies Act, 1956 - Present batch of appeals and writ petition raised questions as to applicability and construction of Section 396 of Act, 1956, which dealt with compulsory amalgamation of companies by a Central Government order, when this became essential in public interest - Whether final amalgamation order was ultra vires Section 396 of the Companies Act, and violative of Article 14 of Constitution of India.

Brief Facts:

The Appellant, 63 Moons Technologies Ltd. (FTIL, which name was changed to 63 Moons Technologies Ltd.), is a 99.99% shareholder of the National Spot Exchange Ltd. (NSEL), and is a listed company. About 45% of the shareholding of FTIL is held by Shri Jignesh Shah and family, and about 43% of the shareholding is held by members of the Indian public. Approximately 5% of the shareholding is held by institutional investors. FTIL is a profitable company, having a positive net worth of over INR

2500 crore, and is in the business of providing software which is used for trading by brokers and exchanges across the country. FTIL has about 900 employees, and a Board of Directors which is different from the Board of Directors of its wholly owned subsidiary, i.e., NSEL. On the other hand, NSEL was incorporated in 2005 by Multi Commodities Exchanges [MCX] and its nominees. Ministry of Finance, Government of India, issued a notification withdrawing the exemption granted to NSEL. Exemptions granted to the National Commodity and Derivatives Exchange Ltd. (NCDEX) Spot Exchange and the National Agricultural Produce Market Committee (APMC) were also withdrawn. Additional Secretary, Department of Economic Affairs, wrote a letter to the Ministry of Corporate Affairs stating that FTIL and NSEL appear to be maintaining separate identities for a fraudulent purpose, i.e., to deprive investors of their money. As a result, there is a need to lift the corporate veil in order to unearth the fraud, as a result of which, amalgamation of two companies, where one has defrauded market participants and the other company is cash-rich and capable of addressing the payment crisis more effectively. It was therefore proposed to merge FTIL and NSEL under Section 396 of the Companies Act. On 21st October, 2014, a draft order of amalgamation, made in accordance with Section 396(3) of the Companies Act, was circulated to the relevant stakeholders. As a result, FTIL filed Writ Petition. Bombay High Court directed the parties to maintain status quo. Union of India filed an affidavit in reply, categorically confirming that the impugned draft order has been made by the Central Government on the basis of the FMC's proposal dated 18.08.2014. Bombay High Court vacated the status quo order, and passed an order allowing FTIL, NSEL, and their shareholders to file their objections to the draft amalgamation order. Meanwhile, Under Section 396(3), a compensation order was made, which involved compensation only to a particular shareholder of NSEL. Central Government issued a notification to merge the functions of the FMC with the Securities and Exchange Board of India [SEBI]. On the same day, the FCRA was also repealed. Thus, SEBI was now vested with the powers of the FMC which is to be governed by the Securities and Exchange Board of India Act, 1992 [SEBI Act]. Final amalgamation order was passed in terms of Section 396(3), thereby merging FTIL and NSEL, wherein all assets and liabilities of NSEL would become assets and liabilities of FTIL.

Held, while allowing the appeal

1. Section 396 cannot be challenged on the ground of Article 14 or Article 19, given Article 31A of the Constitution of India. However, this does not mean that, Section 396 must be construed in such a fashion that, it would lead to arbitrary or unreasonable results. [23]

Section 396(3) speaks of a shareholder's or a creditor's interest in or rights against the company resulting from an amalgamation order. Such "interest in" or "rights against" refers to real and substantive rights, as opposed to rights that are only in form. A shareholder or creditor gets effected by an amalgamation order, if the value of his share gets depleted as a result of the amalgamation and if dividends that have been paid to him are likely to come down as a result of the amalgamation. Likewise, a creditor of a solvent company is directly effected by an amalgamation by which the amount loaned by such creditor becomes, as a result of the amalgamation, less likely to be paid back in time, than if the amalgamation did not take place. Such rights and interests of members and creditors are substantive rights which, when effected by the amalgamation, lead to compensation having to be paid. Every shareholder of a company and indeed, every creditor of a company, is concerned only with the "economic value" of his share or the loan granted to a company, as the case may be. The moment the share value, in real terms, is likely to dip, and/or loans granted are likely not to be repaid in time or at all as a result of an amalgamation, such members or creditors of the amalgamating company are equally entitled to be compensated for this economic loss as are the members and creditors of the amalgamated company, depending on the facts of each case. A reasonable construction must be given to Section 396. [65]

12. Thus, it is clear from a reading of Section 396(3), (3A), and (4)(aa) that, every member or creditor of each of the companies before amalgamation shall have, as nearly as may be, the same interest in or rights against the company resulting from the amalgamation as he had in the original company. To the extent to which the interest or rights of such member or creditor are less than his interest or rights against the original company, post amalgamation, he shall be entitled to compensation which is to be assessed. Post assessment, if such member or creditor is aggrieved, he may prefer an appeal to the appellate authority under Sub-section (3A). Under Sub-section (4)(aa), no order of amalgamation can be made unless the time for preferring an appeal under Sub-section (3A) has expired, or where any such appeal has been preferred, the appeal has been finally disposed of. [66]

13. Fact that, the assessment order dated 1st April, 2015 did not provide any compensation to either the shareholders or creditors of FTIL for the economic loss caused by the amalgamation in breach of Section 396(3), it is clear that an important condition precedent to the passing of the final amalgamation order was not met. On this ground also, therefore, the final amalgamation order has to be held to be ultra vires Section 396 of the Companies Act, and, being arbitrary and unreasonable, violative of Article 14 of the Constitution of India. [74]

14. The order dated 12th February, 2016 is ultra vires Section 396 of the Companies Act, and violative of Article 14 of the Constitution. Appeals allowed. [76]

CHAPTER NINETEEN

Sagufa Ahmed and Ors. vs. Upper Assam Plywood Products Pvt. Ltd. and Ors., 2020

Hon'ble Judges/Coram:

S.A. Bobde, C.J.I., A.S. Bopanna and V. Ramasubramanian, JJ.

Relevant Section:

Section 421(3) of the Companies Act, 2013

Equivalent Citations:

MANU/SC/0697/2020, (5)ALT167, I(2021)BC3(SC), 2020(6)BLJ291, 2020 (4) CCC 46 , [2020]158CLA446(SC), [2020]222CompCas559(SC), 2020(6)CTC420, ILR2020(4)Kerala1, 2020 (5) KHC 89, 2020(4)KLJ584, 2021-1-LW481, (2020)7MLJ92, (2020)200PLR105, 2020(4)RCR(Civil)453, (2021)2SCC317, 2020 (7-8) SCJ 763, [2021]163SCL201(SC)

Case Note:

Company -Appeal - Time barred - Condonation of delay - Section 421(3) of the Companies Act, 2013 - Condonation as sought declined - Instant appeal was filed to challenge NCLT's impugned order after 45 days of limitation period - Appellant cited delay in obtaining free copy of order and also pandemic preventing filing of appeal within time - Appeal however was still filed much after prescribed period of limitation after procuring even the certified copy - Whether the Application for condonation of delay and thus appeal rightly dismissed as time barred? - Hence, the present Appeal

Facts:

The present appeal was filed against the order passed by the National Company Law Appellate Tribunal ('NCLAT') that dismissed an application for condonation of delay as well as an appeal being time barred.The Appellants had moved an application before National Company Law Tribunal ('NCLT') for the winding up of the company, which was dismissed by an order dated 25.10.2019. They applied for a certified copy on 21.11.2019 (as per their claim, whereas the copy application bears the date 22.11.2019). Order copy was received by their counsel on 19.12.2019. Appeal was filed before NCLAT on 20.07.2020 along with an application for condonation of delay. Application was dismissed on the ground that the Tribunal has no power to condone the delay beyond a period of 45 days and consequently the appeal was also dismissed. Hence the present appeal. There were two-fold contentions raised namely (i) that the Appellate Tribunal erred in computing the period of limitation from the date of the order of the NCLT, contrary to Section 421(3) of the Companies Act, 2013, and (ii) that the Appellate Tribunal failed to take note of the lockdown as well as the order passed by this Court on 23.03.2020 in Suo Motu Writ Petition (Civil) No. 3 of 2020, extending the period of limitation for filing any proceeding with effect from 15.03.2020 until further orders.

Held, while dismissing the Appeals:

The period of limitation of 45 days prescribed in Section 421(3) would start running only from the date on which a copy of the order of the Tribunal is made available to the person aggrieved. Under Section 420(3) of the Act read with Rule 50, the Appellants were entitled to be furnished with a certified copy of the order free of cost.[13]

Therefore if the Appellants had chosen not to file a copy application, but to await the receipt of a free copy of the order in terms of Section 420(3) read with Rule 50, they would be perfectly justified in falling back on Section 421(3), for fixing the date from which limitation would start running. But the Appellants in this case, chose to apply for a certified copy after 27 days of the pronouncement of the order in their presence and they now fall back upon Section 421(3).[14]

Despite the above factual position, we do not want to hold against the Appellants, the fact that they waited from 25.10.2019 (the date of the order of NCLT) upto 21.11.2019, to make a copy application. But atleast from 19.12.2019, the date on which a certified copy was admittedly received by the counsel for the Appellants, the period of limitation cannot be stopped from running.[15]

By virtue of the proviso to Section 421(3), the Appellate Tribunal was empowered to condone the delay upto a period of period of 45 days. This period of 45 days started running from 02.02.2020 and it expired even according to the Appellants on 18.03.2020. The Appellants did not file the appeal on or before 18.03.2020, but filed it on 20.07.2020. [17]

To get over their failure to file an appeal on or before 18.03.2020, the Appellants rely upon the order dated 23.03.2020 in Suo Motu Writ Petition (Civil) No. 3 of 2020.[18]

But the Appellants can take refuge under the above order. What was extended by the above order of this Court was only "the period of limitation" and not the period upto which delay can be condoned in exercise of discretion conferred by the statute. The above order passed by this Court was intended to benefit vigilant litigants who were prevented due to the pandemic and the lockdown, from initiating proceedings within the period of limitation prescribed by general or special law.[19]

Therefore, the Appellants cannot claim the benefit of the order passed by this Court on 23.03.2020, for enlarging, even the period up to which delay can be condoned. The second contention is thus untenable. Hence the appeals are liable to be dismissed. Accordingly, they are dismissed.[25]

CHAPTER TWENTY

Navinchandra Steels Private Limited vs. SREI Equipment Finance Limited and Ors., 2021

Hon'ble Judges/Coram:

Rohinton Fali Nariman and B.R. Gavai, JJ.

Relevant Section:

Companies Act, 1956 - Section 446; Section 279, Section 230

Equivalent Citation: 2021(5)ABR809, AIR2021SC1180, 2021(3)ALLMR606, 2021(2)ALT134, II(2021)BC133(SC), 2021(2)BomCR783, 132(2021)CLT264, [2021]225CompCas374(SC), 2021(2)CTC891, (2021)4SCC435, MANU/SC/0130/2021

Case Note:

Insolvency - Corporate Insolvency - Resolution proceedings - Section 7 of the Insolvency and Bankruptcy Code, 2016 (IBC) - Winding proceedings already pending - Maintainability of Resolution Proceedings - It was contended that IBC being a special statute shall prevail - Determination thereof - Whether proceedings under Section 7 of the IBC is independent and to prevail over general statute i.e. Companies Act?

Brief Facts:

The present appeal arose against the judgment passed by the National Company Law Appellate Tribunal [NCLAT]. The Appellant is an operational creditor of Respondent No. 2 (SRUIL), the company under winding up-and has a decree in its favour passed by the Bombay High Court in Summary Suit. Division Bench stayed the order and directed SRUIL to make a deposit or furnish a bank guarantee for the same, failing which the stay order would get vacated. The said appeal is pending. Appellant earlier had filed a winding up petitionagainst SRUIL before the Bombay High Court which is still pending. A winding up petitionfiled by Respondent No. 3 (Action Barter) against SRUIL, by a conditional order stood admitted on the failure of SRUIL to make a deposit. The appeal instituted by SRUIL against this order was dismissed, whereas the appeal instituted by Action Barter was allowed. The parties then filed consent terms before the Single Judge, wherein Action Barter agreed to accept a sum of money payable in instalments. Apart from the payment of the first instalment of INR 25 lakh, no further instalment was paid, as a result of which the winding up petition stood revived and the provisional liquidator took over the physical possession of the assets of SRUIL.While this winding up petition was pending, Indiabulls Housing Finance Ltd. (Indiabulls), a secured creditor of SRUIL, filed a petition under Section 7 of the IBC which was dismissed as being not maintainable as a winding up petition had already been admitted by the Bombay High Court. An appeal to the NCLAT suffered a similar fate. Indiabullssought direction against the Provisional Liquidator to handover physical possession of the Mortgaged Property in question to the Secured Creditor herein, in accordance with and pursuant to the provisions of the Companies Act, 1956 and the Securitisation and Reconstruction of Financial Assets and Enforcement of Security Interest Act, 2002

Held, while dismissing the Appeals:

A conspectus of the aforesaid authorities would show that a petition either Under Section 7 or Section 9 of the IBC is an independent proceeding which is unaffected by winding up proceedings that may be filed qua the same company. Given the object sought to be achieved by the IBC, it is clear that only where a company in winding up is near corporate death that no transfer of the winding up proceeding would then take place to the NCLT to be tried as a proceeding under the IBC. Short of an irresistible conclusion that corporate death is inevitable, every effort should be made to resuscitate the corporate debtor in the larger public interest, which includes not only the workmen of the corporate debtor, but also its creditors and the goods it produces in the larger interest of the economy of the country. [23]

The secured creditor is outside the winding up and can realise his security without the leave of the winding up Court, though if he files a suit or takes other legal proceedings for the realisation of his security he is bound under Section 231 (corresponding with Section 171 of the

Indian Companies Act) to obtain the leave of, the winding up Court before he can do so although such leave would almost automatically be granted. The provisions in Section 317 are also supplementary to the provisions of Section 231 and emphasise the position of the secured creditor as one outside the winding up, the secured creditor being, in regard to the exercise of those rights and privileges, in the same position as he would be under the Bankruptcy Act.[25]

Indiabulls, a secured creditor of the corporate debtor has in enforcement of its debt by a mortgage, sold the mortgaged property outside the winding up. The aforesaid sale is the subject matter of proceedings in the Bombay High Court filed by the provisional liquidator. If the aforesaid sale is set aside, the asset of SRUIL that has been sold will come back to the provisional liquidator for the purposes of winding up. If the sale is upheld, equally, there are other assets of SRUIL which continue to be in the hands of the provisional liquidator for the purposes of winding up. Though no application for transfer of the winding up proceeding pending in the Bombay High Court has been filed, the Bombay High Court has itselfdirected the provisional liquidator to hand over the records and assets of SRUIL to the IRP in the Section 7 proceeding that is pending before the NCLT.[26]

Appeal dismissed

Rapid Metro Rail Gurgaon Limited and Ors. vs. Haryana Mass Rapid Transport Corporation Limited and Ors., 2021

Hon'ble Judges/Coram:
Dr. D.Y. Chandrachud, M.R. Shah and Sanjiv Khanna, JJ.
Relevant Sections:
Companies Act, 2013 - Section 130, Section 241(2), Section 242
Equivalent Citation:
2021(223)AIC129, MANU/SC/0223/2021
Case Notes:
Company - Debt due - Financial audit - Second Respondent entered into Concession Agreement with Appellant No. 1 for execution of Project No. 1 on design, build, finance, operate and transfer basis - Respondent granted concession to appellant for period of ninety nine years - Respondent executed another Concession Agreement with appellant no.2 for execution of Project No. 2 - Appellants completed Projects, in meantime, all metro projects and projects would gave to first Respondent - Appellants issued notice of termination to second respondent seeking to bring end to Concession Agreement - Appellants wrote to second respondent intimating that divestment requirements contained in Concession Agreement had already been completed by it - However, second respondent had failed to fulfill its obligations to verify Appellants' compliance with such divestment

requirements - NCLAT issued directions for entities, inasmuch as that they had to seek approval of former judge who was appointed to supervise resolution process, before alienating or creating third party rights on assets - Appellants presented memorandum to former judge to seek his approval for handover of Projects to respondents - Respondents issued notice of termination to appellants of Concession Agreement and directed appellants to handover Projects to respondent - Thereafter, former judge permitted appellants to handover possession and control of Projects to respondents - Respondents instituted Writ Petition before High Court challenging notice of termination issued by appellant - Directions were issued by Division Bench recording that consensus had been arrived at in presence of senior officers of contesting parties that Appellants decided to continue Operation and Maintenance of both metro lines - And, as far as debt due was concerned, direction was issued to Comptroller and Auditor General of India (CAG) to appoint team of auditors for financial audit of debt due - In pursuance of order of High Court, CAG filed Application, together with compliance affidavit, before High Court and report was submitted in sealed cover - CAG report adverts to scope of audit which was undertaken in respect of debt due under Concession Agreement - Respondents filed objections to audit report - Proceedings then came up before High Court, when on request of Petitioners before High Court, hearing was deferred - Hence, present appeal - Whether report of financial audit of debt due was complete and conclusive as per scope of audit as decided by CAG.

Brief Facts:

The second Respondent entered into a Concession Agreement with appellant no.1 for the execution of Project No. 1 on a design, build, finance, operate and transfer basis. Second Respondent granted a concession to appellant for a period of ninety nine years from the effective date, including the exclusive right, license and authority during the subsistence of the Concession Agreement to implement and operate Project No. 1. The second respondent issued another RFQ/RFP for developing a metro rail link for Project No. 2. The bid submitted by the consortium was accepted by second respondent, which issued a letter of award. Pursuant to the letter of award, the consortium promoted and incorporated the second Appellant which would fulfill the obligations and exercise the rights of the consortium under the letter of award. Thereafter, a Concession Agreement was entered into between second respondent and appellant no.2 for the execution of Project No. 2. The Appellants completed Projects and in the meantime, the Town and Country Planning Department of the Government directed that all metro projects and projects in the State would be handled by the first Respondent. The appellants issued a notice of termination to second respondent seeking to bring an end to the Concession Agreement. Further, the Appellants responded to the letter of second respondent complaining of material breaches alleged to have been committed by the Appellants under their respective Concession Agreements. The appellants wrote to second respondent intimating that the divestment requirements contained in the Concession Agreement had already been completed by it. However, second respondent had failed to fulfill its obligations to verify appellants's compliance with such divestment requirements. NCLAT issued directions for the entities which had been categorized in the red category, inasmuch as that they had to seek the approval of former judge who was appointed to supervise resolution process before alienating, encumbering, transferring or creating third party rights on assets. Appellants presented a memorandum to former judge to seek his approval for handover of the Projects. The Respondents issued a notice of termination under the Concession Agreement. Terminating the agreement, they directed appellants to handover Projects to first respondent. The former judge permitted appellants to handover possession and control of Projects pursuant to the termination of the Concession Agreement. The Respondents instituted a Writ Petition before the High Court challenging notice of termination issued by appellant, inter alia, on the ground that the period of ninety days shall start from the date of permission, which had not been yet granted by former judge. The directions were issued by the Division Bench recording that a consensus had been arrived at in the presence of senior officers of the contesting parties by which appellants had decided to continue the Operation and Maintenance of both the metro lines. As far as debt due as defined under the concession contract is concerned, direction was issued to the Comptroller and Auditor General of India (CAG) to appoint a team of auditors for the financial audit of the debt due and also for examining the scope of the audit of debt due audited by the second respondent with the assistance of the auditors appointed by the parties to the lis. The High Court allowed an extension of seven days for implementing the directions issued in its orders. In pursuance of the order of the High Court, the Comptroller and Auditor General of India, filed a Civil Miscellaneous Application, together with the compliance affidavit, before the High Court, stating that it had appointed a firm of chartered accountants, to undertake a financial audit of the debt due and sealed report was filed. Thereafter, an affidavit was filed before the High Court by the Advisor (Planning) on behalf of the Respondents, objecting to the audit report. The Division Bench of the High Court noted the affidavit that had been filed by the respondent no.1 and took the affidavit on record, while also noting the submission of appellants that the matter did not brook any delay. The hearing was then adjourned to facilitate filing of replies. The proceedings then came up before the High Court, when on the request of the counsel for the Petitioners before the High Court, the hearing was deferred.

Held, while disposing off the appeal:

The course of events indicates that the entire order which was passed by the High Court was the outcome of sustained negotiations which took place between first and second appellant on the one hand, and respondents on the other, commencing from the invocation of the writ jurisdiction under Article 226. It was significant to note that recourse to the proceedings under Article 226 was taken by respondents, which challenged the termination notice and sought the continuation of the operation of the rapid metro lines which were under imminent threat of closure, once the notice period expired. The narration of events would make it abundantly clear that initially as a result of the order of stay granted by the High Court and thereafter consequent upon mutual discussions, appellants agreed to operate the rapid metro link Projects within which period the handover would take place. Equally, the concerns by appellants, as concessionaires, was that in terms of the Concession Agreements, eight per cent of the debt due had to be deposited in the Escrow Account in terms of the provisions contained in in Concession Agreement. All the parties specifically agreed before the High Court that there would be a reference to the CAG for conducting an audit for the purpose of determining the debt due. The High Court by its order, issued directions which were specifically noted to be emanating from the consensus arrived at in the presence of senior officers of both the parties. [44]

(ii) The directions contained in the High Court's consent order makes it abundantly clear that the audit team appointed by CAG was to conduct a financial audit of the debt due and to examine the scope of the audit. The next important aspect of the consent order was the time bound process which was envisaged, with the audit being completed within thirty days and eighty per cent of the debt due being deposited within thirty days after the receipt of the audit report. The final aspect which needs to be emphasized was that the rest of the disputes between the parties arising out of the audit report were to be agitated in arbitration. [45]

The intervention of this Court under Article 136 of the Constitution was sought having regard to the manner in which the proceedings before the High Court were being derailed. After respondent filed its affidavit, the High Court noted the Appellant's submission that the matter does not brook any delay" and yet adjourned the matter. Thereafter, when the proceedings came up, and the response filed by CAG was taken on the record, the hearing of the writ petitions was again deferred. This course of events indicates that the whole object and purpose behind setting down the timelines in the order stood the risk of being defeated. This Court had been constrained to intervene in the process in order to ensure that the sanctity of the understanding that was arrived at before the High Court was duly maintained. There was a vital public interest element in ensuring that monies which were liable to be deposited in the Escrow Account with a nationalised bank are duly deposited. Respondents, it must be emphasized, were not left without remedy. The deposit into the Escrow Account had to be maintained in that form and will abide by such orders that may be passed by NCLAT or by a competent statutory authority. Besides this, the Concession Agreements provides a clear-cut remedy for seeking reliefs under the arbitration agreement. [58]

(vii) The invocation of the writ jurisdiction of the High Court under Article 226 of the Constitution by respondents was to challenge the termination notices and to obviate the consequence of the cessation of the rapid metro operations, which would have ensued on the expiry of the notice period. The arbitration Clause of the Concession Agreements provides sufficient recourse to remedies which can be availed of. That apart, the order of the High Court had also clarified that the rest of the dispute that remains after the deposit of eighty per cent of the debt due, either arising out of the CAG report, the validity of the termination notices issued by both the parties and any past or future inter se claims and liabilities shall be agitated and decided in the arbitration proceedings. In view of the order which this court propose to pass, the dispute between the High Court in the writ jurisdiction under Article 226 of the Constitution shall stand worked out by granting liberty to the parties to avail of their rights and remedies in accordance with law. [59]

Videos & Tv Shows On Law & Exim

List of some important videos & TV shows on Law & EXIM by Adv. Jayprakash Somani on his YouTube Channel 'Jayprakash Somani EXIM & Legal'

Legal Videos: Hindi -English

1) SLP in Supreme Court / Special Leave Petitions in the Supreme Court of India

2) Transfer of Civil & Criminal Cases by the Supreme Court of India / Transfer of Matrimonial Cases

3) Appellate Jurisdiction of the Supreme Court of India

4) Jurisdictions of the Supreme Court of India

5) Public Interest Litigation in the Supreme Court of India / PIL in Supreme Court

6) Article 32 Writ Petitions in the Supreme Court of India

7) Bail Matters Top 10 Supreme Court Cases

8) FIR Quashing in High Court & Supreme Court

9) Bail & Anticipatory Bail Matters in Supreme Court

10) Insolvency & Bankruptcy Matters in the Supreme Court

11) Insolvency & Bankruptcy Code 2016 Part 1

12) Insolvency & Bankruptcy Code 2016 Part 2

13) Insolvency & Bankruptcy Code 2016 Part 3

14) Corporate Liquidation Process

15) Supreme Court Rules & Procedures Webinar of 2.5 hour on Zoom

16) RDDBFI Act, 1993 (Introduction)

17) The Indian Contact Act 1872

18) Negotiable Instruments Act (Introduction)

19) How to avoid matrimonial disputes& some more videos

20) SEBI Matters in the Supreme Court

21) Matrimonial Matters: Supreme Court's 20 Case Laws

22) Consumer Matters Supreme Court's 20 Case Laws

23) Service Matters Supreme Court's 20 Case Laws

24) How to Search Lawyer for Your Matter

25) Property Matters Supreme Court's 20 Case Laws

26) Bail Matters: Supreme Court's 20 Case Laws

27) Supreme Court / High Court Vacation Benches

28) 69000 Teacher's Recruitment Matters of UP Government in the Supreme Court

29) Contempt of Court Matters in the Supreme Court

30) Advocate Act's Matters in the Supreme Court

31) Business Law Matters in the Supreme Court

32) Banking Matters in the Supreme Court

33) Labour Law Matters in the Supreme Court

34) Arbitration Matters in the Supreme Court

35) Careers in Law -Zoom Webinar by Adv. Jayprakash Somani

36) Civil Matters in the Supreme Court

37) Consumer Protection Act | Consumer Matters in the Supreme Court

38) Corporate Matters in the Supreme Court

39) Criminal Matters in the Supreme Court

40) Role of Respondent in the Supreme Court of India

41) Motor Vehicle Accident Matters in Supreme Court with case laws

42) Article 131 Original Suits in Supreme Court

43) PIL in Supreme Court/ Public Interest Litigations in the Supreme Court of India'

44) CAB Citizenship Amendment Bill is not Unconstitutional

45) Supreme Court of India Cases & Process – Marathi

46) Legal Services Export / Export of Legal Services

47) Transfer of Matrimonial Cases by the Supreme Court of India

48) Public Interest Litigation PIL

49) The Specific Relief Act (Introduction)

50) Corporate Insolvency Resolution Process CIRP

51) ABMM's Career 5 - Careers in Law

52) Transfer of cases by Supreme Court

53) Writ Petitions in High Court & Supreme Court of India

54) Supreme Court Jurisdictions - Appeals, SLP, Writ Petitions, Transfer, Original, Review, Curative

55) LEGAL INDIA TV Show: Cases Handled in Supreme Court

56) Corporate Liquidation Process

57) Legal Services Export / Export of Legal Services

EXIM Videos: Hindi -English

1) Yes, I can do Import Export Business Easily! 36 points excellent video in Hindi

2) Yes, I can do Import Export Business Easily! 36 points excellent video in English

3) Import Export Business – Hindi video

4) Import Export Business - English video

5) Export Import Marathi TV Interview

6) Scope for Commerce Students in International Business- TV Show

7) Scope for Management Student in International Business- TV Show

8) Scope for Engineering Students in International Business – TV Show

9) Women in International Business- TV Show

10) How to do Import Export Business Successfully!'

11) Where one can get full information on Import Export Business?

12) What to do import & export?

13) Import Export Workshop/ Training/Course/ Diploma

14) How to Start Import Export Business & How to grow it. Live Webinar

15) Success Stories & Failure Stories in Import & Export Business

16) For MSME Scope in Export & Import...

17) Exports In Agri. & Food Products – English & some more videos

18) Exports to Dubai, Aabudhabii. e. UAE

19) Jewelry Exports from India

20) How to attend EXIM workshop to become excellent Exporter

21) Import Export Best Training Course – Online & Offline

22) Agri Product Export

23) Scope for Woman in International Business

24) Management Graduates Scope in International Business

25) Pharma Product's Export

26) Best Import Export Course | Practical Training | Aaronica Global Exim

27) Import Export Business for Commerce Graduates

28) How Do I Get Export Orders? Finding International Buyers

29) What Is APEDA In Import Export Business?

30) Which Is The Best Product To Export From India?

31)EXIM Remark by Manoj Kumar Faridabad

32)EXIM Remarks by Mahesh Telangana

33) What Licenses I Need To Start Import/ Export?

34) How Can I Increase My Import Export Business?

35) Which Is Best B2B Website For Import/Export Business?

36) Export Import Management with Global Marketing

37)How to Start Export Import Business | 51 Points Video

38)Scope for Commerce & Other Graduates in International Business

39)BE A SUCCESSFUL EXPORTER FOR OUR NATION - Marathi video

40)Export of Textile , Cotton, Agri., Food, & other products & services

41)Exports from MP, CG, MH, GJ & CA in Fresh Fruits & Vegetables

42)Exports in Agri. & Food Products- Hindi

43)Start your Online/E-Commerce Business

44)How to Start Export Import Business & Grow it

45)Exports in Textile & Other Products

46)Start and grow EXIM business - Live English Webinar

47)'Import Export Business!' Why, Who, What & How can one do it easily!!

48)Live: Export of Product & Services During & After Lock Down Period

49)Frauds in Import Export Business

50)Import Export for Business Man

51)Import & Export for Women

51)Import & Export for Graduate & Post - Graduate Students

52)Agriculture Exports from India

53)Digital Marketing Setup - Marathi

54)2nd Secret of Successful Businessman

55)Digital Marketing Set up

56)Legal Services Export / Export of Legal Services

57)Export & Import with UAE

58)Service Exports / Exports by Service Providers

59)Import Export Workshop/ Training/Course/ Diploma

60)Exports & Imports with USA

61)Selection on Product for Export

62)Top Products Exported from India

63) What to do import & export?

64)ABMM Career 2 - 'Careers in Business & Industries

65) How to do Import Export Business Successfully!'

66)5 Secrets of Successful Businessman

67)Export from MP, Chhattisgarh & Vidarbha Nagpur

68)EXIM Hindi - Textile & Apparel Export

69)EXIM Hindi - Export Import Practical Training In Delhi, Kolkata, Mumbai and Pune

70)Import Export Business

71) Import Export Business Hindi

72) Import Export Business English video

73) Import Export Business Marathi

74) Women in International Business by Exim Guru Adv. Jayprakash Somani

75) Opportunities in Foreign Trade- Adv. Jayprakash Somani's special interview

List Of Adv. Jayprakash Somani's Books

1. Supreme Court of India's Leading Case Laws on 'Insolvency & Bankruptcy Code 2016'
2. Bail Matters – Supreme Court's Latest Leading Case Laws
3. Arbitration Matters- Supreme Court's Latest Leading Case Laws
4. Property Matters - Supreme Court's Latest Leading Case Laws
5. Matrimonial Matters- Supreme Court's Latest Leading Case Laws
6. Election Matters- Supreme Court's Latest Leading Case Laws
7. SEBI Matters- Supreme Court's Latest Leading Case Laws
8. Banking Matters- Supreme Court's Latest Leading Case Laws
9. Service Matters- Supreme Court's Latest Leading Case Laws
10. Contempt of Court Matters- Supreme Court's Latest Leading Case Laws
11. Consumer Protection Matters- Supreme Court's Latest Leading Case Laws
12. Corporate Law- Supreme Court's Latest Leading Case Laws
13. Supreme Court's AOR Exam- Leading Cases
14. Armed Force Tribunal - Supreme Court's Latest Leading Case Laws
15. Acquittal From 376 - Supreme Court's Latest Leading Case Laws
16. Negotiable instrument – Supreme Court's Latest Leading Case Laws
17. Contract Act- Supreme Court's Latest Leading Case Laws
18. Insider trading- Supreme Court's Latest Leading Case Laws
19. Foreign Exchange and Management Act- Supreme Court's Latest Leading Case Laws
20. Income Tax Act- Supreme Court's Latest Leading Case Laws
21. Company Law- Supreme Court's Latest Leading Case Laws
22. Competition & Monopoly Matters- Supreme Court's Latest Leading Case Laws
23. Compassionate Appointment- Service Matters- Supreme Court's Latest Leading Case Laws
24. Compulsory Retirement- Service Matters- Supreme Court's Latest Leading Case Laws
25. Voluntary Retirement- Service Matters- Supreme Court's Latest Leading Case Laws

26. Removal/Dismissal/Termination from Service- Supreme Court's Latest Leading Case Laws
27. Seniority- Service Matter- Supreme Court's Latest Leading Case Laws
28. Promotion- Service Matter- Supreme Court's Latest Leading Case Laws
29. Equal Pay for Equal Work- Service Matter- Supreme Court's Latest Leading Case Laws
30. Condition of Service- Service Matter- Supreme Court's Latest Leading Case Laws
31. Customs Act- Supreme Court's Leading Case Laws
32. Information Technology Act- Supreme Court's Latest Leading Case Laws

These Books are available online at

1. **Notion Press:** https://notionpress.com/author/jayprakash_somani
2. **Amazon:** https://www.amazon.in/s?k=jayprakash+somani
3. **Flipkart:** https://www.flipkart.com/search?q=Jayprakash%20Somani